Children for Social Change:

education for citizenship of street and working children in Brazil

by Anthony Swift

Educational Heretics Press

Published 1997 by Educational Heretics Press
113 Arundel Drive, Bramcote Hills, Nottingham NG9 3FQ

**Educational Heretics Press exists to question the dogmas
of education in general, and schooling in particular.**

**British Cataloguing in Publication Data.
A catalogue record for this book is available
from the British Library.**

Swift, Anthony
Children for Social Change:
education for citizenship of street and working children in Brazil

ISBN   1-900219-09-3

Design and production: Educational Heretics Press

Cover design: Alan Hughes

Photography: Anthony Swift

Printed by Mastaprint Ltd., Sandiacre, Nottinghamshire

Cover photographs:
         Front: Delegates at the 4th National Meeting of Street Boys and
                      Girls in Brasilia.
         Rear: An iced-lolly seller, in Recife

Contents

Note on the author

Anthony Swift is co-author of *Broken Promise - The World of Endangered Children*, and author of *Brazil: the fight for childhood in the cities* and two other books on social issues. He took part in a study for UNICEF-Brazil into the social mobilisation for children's rights and has made a number of visits to programmes working with street and other poor community children. Formerly a journalist in South Africa, he wrote, among other issues, about the impact of apartheid on peoples' lives and about child abuse and neglect. In the UK, he has worked for Third World development funding agencies and is an occasional contributor to *The Guardian, The New Internationalist* and other publications.

Introduction

As I write this introduction, Britain is in one of its increasingly frequent spasms of angst about its children. The epicentre of agitation this time is not the killing of a child by another, or by some deranged adult, nor the systematic sexual abuse of children in the state care system, but a threatened strike by teachers demanding the exclusion from their school of violent and uncontrollable pupils. In the past year alone, we learn 13,419 children were permanently excluded from schools in the UK, adding to the 100,000 or so disaffected young people said to be growing up marginalised from society, many of them drifting into criminality[1].

In the brief tumult of words, admonishments and articles that followed the teachers' action, blame has been cast liberally about - at the teachers themselves, the children, their parents, the church, under-investment in education, disintegration of the family, lack of discipline and the lack of a moral lead. Recommendations have included moral instruction for children, punishment of children - ranging from a slap in time to the return to corporal punishment - fines for parents of reprehensible children and even the electronic tagging of persistent truants aged ten and upwards.

Scarcely a word has been breathed of the two unfashionable experiences children need most - love and respect. It is as though, in our consumer and market focused culture, the very terms are lost to us, let alone how we might accomplish what they stand for.

A curious consolation for me in all of this, is that it may explain why I have found the subject of my book so hard to get to grips with. *Children for Social Change* is about an innovative way of working with socially excluded children developed in Brazil. Better known for that ultimate expression of the exclusion of troublesome children of the underclass - their elimination by death squads - Brazil is also home to the most concerted effort to encourage their participation and organisation. Activists, known as street educators, lay the foundation for this work by setting out to give children the experience of being loved, respected and included.

---

[1] *The Dropout Society: Young People on the Margin*, Clive Wilkinson, Young Minds Magazine, January 1996.

The exclusion of children from a school is never a single or even simple chain of events, as some of the remedies proposed recently in the UK would seem to imply. Teachers' demands for their expulsion contribute to a complex experience of rejection in which many people will have had a hand and which is likely to have been partly determined even before the children were born, with the social rejection of their parents. It is not by chance that boys of Afro-Caribbean origin in the UK are six times more likely to be excluded than white boys, or that certain categories of white boys are probably more likely to be excluded than others. In Brazil, the majority of street and criminalised children are among the descendants of the country's massive former slave population, the ultimately excluded class, upon whose backs concentrations of great private wealth were built. Their exclusion is clearly part of the broader relegation of people to an underclass.

What Brazil's street educators do, quite unlike the UK teachers who threatened to strike, is assume a personal responsibility for reversing the social exclusion of the children they work with. By engaging with them, instead of accepting their abandonment, they forge a new social alliance that is mutually and socially transforming. Being loved, valued and included, the children are able to become critically aware of the processes that consign them and their families, among 32 million fellow Brazilians, to live in poverty. Instead of being made victims of these processes, or of recreating them, many become, in various ways and degrees, protagonists for social change.

A vigorous National Movement of Street Boys and Girls has emerged, whose members - poor community children and educators - have taken a prominent role in defining children's rights and responsibilities, securing legal rights and developing an educational experience through which both educator and child learn to exercise citizenship.

I found this translation of work with children into a new political force also hard to grasp. Here was utopian political action, based not on wishful thinking but on an experience of a common humanity, created daily through relationships that challenge, and are challenged by, the established norm.

In writing about something so radically opposed to the 'free' market values that, for over 15 years, have dominated our thought and actions, determining the very language we use and with it our conceptual framework, I have been dogged by terminological problems. Should I write of 'love and respect' - even though we no longer know what they mean - or perhaps resort to the more measured Rogerian phrase 'unconditional positive regard'? I decided to invest in the older terms, which the people involved themselves use. Would such phrases as 'social exclusion' or 'social rejection' convey the process that relegates people to the underclass, or should I employ the term, 'marginalisation', still relatively unfamiliar outside Latin America? In fact I have used all three almost interchangeably. Should I borrow J.K. Galbraith's concept of the 'Culture of Contentment', identifying the self-absorption of the modern consumer classes whose pursuit of personal well-being at the expense of others helps generate the excluding society? I have referred instead to 'combat culture' or 'culture of domination' in an attempt to indicate the underlying scramble for personal well-being that determines those choices and precludes the possibility of our discovering well-being as contributors to the community.

As an agnostic, I anticipated another realm of terminological difficulty arising from the fact that the work of street educators was conceived within a religious framework, albeit that of liberation theology where socialism and Christianity most readily converge. Some educators who are militants of liberation theology regard what they are doing as working to 'realise the Kingdom of God on Earth' or to 'rescue the Christ who is in all of us'. However, they do not use such terms dogmatically and are talking about consciously rescuing or resurrecting our essential humanity amid the forces that would deny it. For them the work is a celebration of faith. For me and doubtless the many non-Christian educators it is just one of the best ideas around.

My primary aim in writing *Children for Social Change* was to introduce the Brazilian experience to other front-line workers with poor community children in other industrialised and Third World countries. Since it is about people who have developed different educational goals and a different methodology from those offered by conventional schools, it may also be of interest to teachers. It should also interest students of such thinker/practitioners as Paulo Freire, Don Bosco, Maria Montessori and Leonardo Boff, whose ideas contributed to the actions described. I think my subject matter also has relevance to the host of people who, like me, are trying to recover some sense of community and individual purpose following the social vandalism of the Thatcher-Reagan era.

I set out seeking the crock of gold at the heart of the children's movement in Brazil, guided unwittingly by the journalistic fallacy of our times that distinguishes only between extraordinary and merely ordinary people. I wanted to expose a social process by writing about a remarkable proponent of it.

However the subject - who, with a group of poor community youth and children on the streets of Belém, founded the Republic of Small Vendors 25 years ago - would not let me. Padre Bruno Sechi deflected my attention back to the work itself and the multitude of people involved in it, allowing me to discover no saints but a widely distributed human propensity for good and for resistance to what threatens to destroy our more humane inclinations.

In trying to convey something of the development of the children's movement in Brazil, I have largely focused at a local level on the Movement of the Republic of Emmaus (formerly the Republic of Small Vendors) and related its work to the National Movement of Street Boys and Girls. I chose the Movement of the Republic of Emmaus because it has been a key pioneer of the participation and organisation of poor community children and because I believed I might gain in depth of insight what I lost by taking a narrower focus. Thanks to earlier research visits, I have been able to draw on experience of other programmes in São Paulo, Rio de Janeiro, Belo Horizonte, Goiânia, Recife and Brasilia.

The Movement of the Republic of Emmaus is, of course, just one tributary of the National Movement, whose membership is made up of several thousand educators and children located in a host of local movements and organisations around the country. In addition, the National Movement has more than 100 associate member organisations, which identify with its core principles and methodology, while at the same time demonstrating a wide variety of approach, determined by local conditions and the people involved.

Some of these organisations create scarcely any infrastructure, concentrating on street-level work and instead putting the children in touch with what resources are available in the community. Others have created complex structures. The Movement of the Republic of Emmaus is among the latter. In addition to its street and community-level work, it recycles donated goods, offers employment and occupational training, provides a range of sports, games and other activities, operates a multi-disciplinary health clinic, has established a pioneering community school, an agricultural production unit, a herbal remedies nursery and dispensary, a children's legal defence centre and even a news agency, reporting on children's rights issues throughout Amazonia. It also has a distinctive mobilising approach of engaging youth from poor communities in the work with children on the street, rather than recruiting experienced educators. Its educators are trained before and on the job and, through their work with the children, enter into a dynamic relationship in which both learn and undergo a distinct change of orientation and outlook. While some educators stay with the Republic, or continue as educators elsewhere, many, like the children themselves, go on to different activities, occupations and areas of social action, taking their formative experience with them.

While there is much to inspire in the work of the Movement of the Republic of Emmaus, its members would be the last to propose it as a model and the first to suggest that there are many other initiatives as interesting. There are few books about such experiences as that of the Movement of the Republic of Emmaus. So much the worse. Hundreds of thousands of groups of people around the world oppose themselves to the forces that relegate people to live in poverty. Much of the money donated to voluntary aid agencies by millions of people in the UK goes to them. But little in-depth information comes back.

The common search for quick-fix answers to urgent social problems may tempt some practicioners to extract and transfer techniques without taking due account of the process by which they were developed. To capture something of the process I attempted an historical approach. This posed its own challenges. Progressive work with poor community children in Brazil today has evolved over more than quarter of a century. It was born in a military dictatorship and continues to take part in the struggle for real democracy, surviving the opening years of neo-liberalism, with its embrace of socially disastrous free market theology, privatisation and downsizing. Through all these phases, the conditions of poverty endured by millions of Brazilians have generally worsened, undermining the potential for voluntary action and making popular resistance more difficult. The movement has survived and continued to realise its goals through the hard work, resourcefulness, imagination and readiness of its participants to reformulate their approach to meet the changing times.

It has been said of the pioneers of the children's movement that they lived books but never wrote them. There was just not the time. I wanted to help remedy that by using whenever possible their own words. What follows is based mainly on interviews with people who helped found the children's movement or have joined it since. On starting to integrate these interviews, I found that people's memories of events did not always quite match. Inevitably, there are some gaps.

I would like to acknowledge the participation of all the people quoted in *Children for Social Change*. Among others who gave me valuable time but are mentioned only fleetingly, or not at all, are João de Deus in São Paulo, Joe McCarthy and Adriano and Helena in Recife. They were the first street educators I encountered back in 1987, and their work immediately caught my interest. Others are Mario Volpi, the third Co-ordinator of the National Movement, who allowed me to sit in at a preparatory workshop of the National Committee of children who planned and staged the Fourth National Meeting; Clébia, from the National Movement in Santarem, who represented the State of Pará at the workshop and who made me a souvenir of Brazil that still stands on my study shelf (she did not make it to the meeting itself because her brother's murder threw her family into crisis); 'King', whom I met some years ago through Joe McCarthy in a favela near Olinda weeks before he was shot dead by a security man for 'stealing' a coconut from a palm; Vesna Bosnjak, of UNICEF Brazil, who has encouraged me in this work; Reinaldo Bulgarelli, who helped pioneer the street educator's role in São Paulo; Antonio Carlos Gomes da Costa, a progressive manager of public policy who has played an important role in the struggle for children's rights; Martinha Arruda, adviser, *companheira* and marathon simultaneous interpreter, who knows as much and probably more than I do about this subject now. I also wish to thank a number of friends not yet mentioned who read through the text and made valuable suggestions - Donatella Velluti, Jo Beall and Barabara Kahan, as well as my wife, Ann Perry. There are many other adults and children who could and should be named - particularly from the Movement of the Republic of Emmaus - who may detect their influence on the pages that follow. Finally I would like to thank the Rowntree Foundation, Misereor and Paddock's Children's Trust for supporting the research for this book.

Anthony Swift,
Oxford, 28th November 1996

"The first and greatest violence is the systematic exclusion of people - a great number of people - by society. From this violence other violence directly and indirectly flows. Where you exclude, you must establish instruments to control those who are excluded so that they don't invade the peace of those who have access to opportunities and wealth."

Padre Bruno Sechi

Chapter one

A passionate wish for social change

It was an inauspicious time for a would-be liberator of the human spirit. Bruno Sechi arrived in Brazil from Sardinia in 1964 at the moment of the military coup. Dictatorship was to have the next 20 years to hammer the old principles of colonial and post-colonial oppression into a new mould of capitalist industrial development. Bruno was headed for the Salesian Institute Pius XI in São Paulo to study for the priesthood. He had faith in the potential for good in people and, like others in the church at the time, was appalled by the wholesale abandonment of human lives to poverty. He was determined to do something about it. He doubted, however, that a vanguard of revolutionaries seizing power could bring about enduring change. It had to come from the passionate wish for liberation in society at large, through a process of social transformation emanating most crucially from the oppressed themselves.

The wellspring of such a wish was there. It was evidenced by a history of people's resistance to their oppression and by the operation in poor communities of besieged social principles deriving from black and Indian cultures. These were the humanitarian principles of co-operation, solidarity, sharing of resources and individual interest identified with that of the community - the antithesis of the prevailing combat culture, in which people pursue personal well-being at the expense and exclusion of others. But how could Bruno as a priest work to strengthen peoples' faith in the former?

In particular, he looked to youth from the excluded classes for a way forward. Discounted on account of their poverty and youth, they were denied both opportunities and respect. Their openness to new experience, their hunger for a cause, tempted him to dream that in them lay possibilities

1

of both their own and a wider transformation. Were they able to reveal their worth, to themselves and others, they might help stiffen the forces of resistance and subvert the prejudice by which the comfortably off tend to justify their rejection of the underclass.

In the name of modernisation, the military regime opened the doors to a state and capitalist programme fuelled by the quest for personal gain at its most rapacious. The abandonment of human lives marginal to the process was set to assume production-line proportions. Brazil was propelled into the world's top-ten economic powers at the cost of abandoning half its population to poverty and one in five to absolute poverty[1]. Rapid urban industrial growth produced widespread social upheaval, enabled a small minority to siphon the nation's wealth into their hands and left the country massively indebted to commercial interests abroad.

Between 1960 and 1980, 40 million subsistence farmers and labouring families were displaced from the land by poverty, or expelled from it by landowners or major capital intensive development schemes - dams and roads - that served the interests of the urban elite. Lured to urban centres by the hope of work and left to fend for themselves, they set up rudimentary shelters in what vacant spaces they could find. Drifts of deprivation accumulated on the peripheries of cities on what became known as "invasion lands". Only a quarter of the population lived in cities 30 years ago. Today the proportion has risen through migration and natural growth to 75%.

From families with the fewest resources[2] in the urban concentrations of poverty, there was to be a growing spillage of adolescents and then children on to city streets. In a process not peculiar to Brazil, a fearful public came to regard them as a threat - as outlaws and bandits. To some people they were no better than vermin, to be eradicated with impunity.

Appealing to the young

The boom in oppressive regimes and human suffering throughout Latin America contributed to a reorientation within the Catholic Church. The 1968 Medellin Conference of Latin American bishops declared a 'preferential option for the poor', opening the way to the development in the

---

[1] Of Brazil's 162 million population, some 32 million live in abject poverty.

[2] Not only financially, but also in terms of knowledge and family and community support.

'70s of liberation theology[3]. The latter hold that only by making common cause with people condemned to poverty, and working out with them a gospel of liberation, might one be accounted a true Christian. People of this persuasion questioned both the abuse of power by politicians and the way the church itself wielded and served power and authority. They wanted to release Christianity from the institution of the church and liberate it in the hearts and actions of people in the community. Instead of offering ameliorating rewards in the hereafter for suffering endured on earth, they sought the resurrection of humanity in an increasingly bitter here and now. For them, the church did not represent a perfectly ordered, hierarchical society, but 'the community of the faithful, living in comradely relationships of sharing, love and service'[4].

An activist[5] describes discovering this new realm of political action within the church: *"In '68 I had participated in the student movement. I had plunged head first into it and discovered the underground left-wing organisations. I avoided the repression and a few years later went back to university. I worked on research about peasants in the interior of the country, and for the first time made direct contact with this reality. I decided to leave the university and work in popular education, and then I made a great discovery. I was sent to offer an advisory service in the interior of the State of Pará in the north of the country. There I encountered work being done by priests, nuns and lay people of the church. I was absolutely amazed: these people had an outlook I had not encountered before. They lived there in the middle of the forest for years, together with the peasants, mixing religion with the political struggle, appearing to be integrated into the population. It was something quite different to the left that I had known. At the time, it seemed to me to be a new option."*

Priests and nuns who identified with this process began to dismantle their institutional aloofness and relate on a more equal footing to lay people. There was a proliferation of popular pastoral missions and of widely varied community initiatives - mothers' clubs, reflection groups, bible study groups, credit co-operatives, community vegetable gardens. This assistance work led to the development of Basic[6] Christian Communities whose members

---

[3]*Introducing Liberation Theology*, by Leonardo Boff, Colodovis Boff, Burns and Oats.
[4]Ibid page 59.
[5]The friend who culled this quote has unfortunately mislaid the source.
[6]The term refers to the social base, whose labour and deprivation support the pyramid of privilege.

associated bible study with action in society. Many of these communities were led not by priests but trained lay people. In the makeshift impoverished districts of cities where migrants accumulated, they initiated schemes to build better homes, or lobby the municipalities for services - such as access to water and public transport.

As the regime cracked down on its opponents with increasing brutality, it became impossible to hold meetings, or even talk politics openly. Trade union activity was tightly controlled. Activists were forced underground. Many went into exile, some into the armed struggle. A large number took shelter under the umbrella of the church and continued to resist the oppression by engaging in small-scale grassroots projects in the community.

Poor community organisations and movements mushroomed. There were 80,000 Basic Christian Communities alone with an estimated membership of two million. These initiatives helped define a new social identity - that of the spirited, hard-working activist, outraged by social injustice, self-denying and seeking solidarity with his or her fellow oppressed[7]. This shared morality united, and continues to unite, activists in a wide variety of church and agnostic movements striving for social justice - workers, landless labourers, black people - making possible the concept of a broad popular movement. In time, people identifying with these values were to transform the trade union movement, making it a key player in Brazil's struggle for democratic government.

Bruno Sechi was at one with the new expressions of resistance. As a young seminarian, his championing of new church practice nearly cost him the priesthood. He was accused of organising a protest among fellow seminarians demanding the application of new rules of the Council of Vatican Two. As punishment, he was barred from qualifying with his fellow students. When he persisted in his studies the following year and there was no denying him his ordination, he was assigned to a pastorate in the periphery of a small town inland of São Paulo, under the authority of an arch-conservative bishop.

Undaunted, he set about initiating new practice, relying on winning over his opponents with the results rather than asking permission beforehand. He gave his first mass in Portuguese instead of Latin, facing instead of

---

[7] *Brazil - Carnival of the Oppressed, Lula and the Brazilian Workers' Party*, by Sue Branford and Bernardo Kucinski, LAB, 1995.

4

presenting his back to his congregation. These elementary steps in closing the gap between priest and community attracted many youngsters into the church, softening conservative opposition in the congregation. With the crushing of the students' movement by the military regime, church youth groups began to spring up around the country. In working with youth for the first time, Padre Bruno helped form a group that developed a strong sense of solidarity and became enduringly active in social issues.

Towards the end of the '60s, he moved on to join the Salesian Occupational College in Sacramenta, a poor district in the City of Belém, capital of the State of Pará, in the north of the country. It was the fifth year of military rule when repression was entering its most intense phase and the culture of authoritarianism pervaded all aspects of life, including the home.

Run by Italians, the college was progressive in some ways and very traditionalist in others. Male and female students were strictly segregated, their classes held in separate buildings on either side of a road. Any girl dispatched on an errand to the boys' school, caused a sensation. Girls and boys would attend mass marshalled by nuns and priests to opposite sides of the church. In a radical action at the time, Padre Bruno set about dismantling this gender apartheid. His concern was that it was unnatural and inhibited the equal participation of the sexes and free exchange of ideas. Proposing the introduction of a youth mass, he insisted on free seating, a liberating experience for the young people concerned. The tone of the mass was joyful and celebratory, enlivened by the music of young guitarists, further challenging traditionalists in the congregation. The chatter and laughter of youngsters coming into the church attacked the atmosphere of solemnity. For Padre Bruno such noise was a sign of life. An elderly priest, later a key supporter, fled the building, slamming the doors behind him.

The young flocked to the new mass. Afterwards they would gather informally to discuss social, religious and the personal issues of particular interest to the young people - sexuality, falling in love, dating and marriage, what families were about. They would also consider how they should apply the messages of the gospel to everyday life.

From this process a particular group began to form. Most of those involved were from poor backgrounds, but when they first began to participate in the youth-mass meetings they were upwardly mobile. *"We were young and gave no thought to the districts we lived in, or people in poverty,"* recalls Graça Trapasso, a member of the group, and a person full of life and bounce.

5

"Our main thought was to escape poverty. I was 17. We all had jobs or were preparing to go to university and get better jobs. Some of us joined the youth meetings at first just to have a good time - to play together, to go dancing. It was the time of 'Yeah, Yeah, Yeah' and smoking grass. Because Padre Bruno started encouraging us to read, to listen to music, to discuss the gospel and relate it to the world we lived in, we discovered that Christ was not that statue in the church which had little to do with us. He was a man in a society very like our own who took the side of people who lived in poverty. And we began asking, 'Who are these people?' Instead of thinking about how we could put poverty behind us, we began asking, 'Why should people be excluded from society? Hadn't they as much right to be a part of it as anyone else? And what ought we do about it?' "

In these discussions Padre Bruno was developing his own skills as a facilitator. Just as he disbelieved the prevailing assumption that people with political and economic power knew what was best for those without, he strongly doubted the precept that adults automatically knew what was best for young people and children. What interested him was the idea of children and youth themselves realising their own possibilities, and for that to happen a new educational approach was needed.

"After those masses and debates, we wanted to fix up the world," recalls Jaime Cabral de Silva, another member of the original group. *"We were developing a critical consciousness. You couldn't talk politics openly but, by reflecting on the gospel, we were dealing with political issues. We began to feel that masses and meetings were not enough. We had to do something that would contribute to changing society. Our political consciousness then grew further through the action we took."*

"Padre Bruno had ambitious dreams of changing society. And he passed them on to us," said another group member. *"We wanted to bring about change but to do it by raising awareness rather than provoking opposition."*

Parallel to the youth meetings, Padre Bruno was being consulted by adults, usually couples, who wanted to live according to their faith. The couples were of different social classes and occupations, including professional people. Some of them occasionally joined the youth group in their discussions, contributing specialised knowledge or experience. They were to form an important network of sympathisers who in time helped mobilise wider support in the city for the work developed by the youth.

6

The youth mass and meetings became immensely popular. Even upper-middle-class families began sending their children along in the expectation that they would undergo some kind of a spiritual conversion. This development threatened to change the nature of the meetings and they were abandoned in 1970. But by then a core group of about 25 young people had formed. What marked them out from other young groups in Belém at the time was their interest in applying Christian values to everyday life.

The forming of a group of young activists

Instead of simply meeting, the core-group members started participating in weekend community experiences, intensifying their relationship. Held at Salesian College, the communal weekends would start on a Friday evening and go through to Monday morning. Sometimes the group would go instead on a camping expedition to an island in the Amazon estuary owned by a well-wisher.

By common consent, all tasks - cooking, cleaning - were shared, the young people volunteering with an enthusiasm rarely demonstrated in their own homes. Discussion, reflection and other activities, such as reading and games, frequently extended into the early hours. *"This development was very exciting for us,"* said Graça Trapasso, one of the core group. *"Until then, everything new and interesting seemed to be happening far away from us in the big centres. We were always waiting for new ideas to get to us. So before the group was formed, we didn't feel we belonged anywhere."* Though the girls slept in separate quarters from the boys, the intimacy of the group so worried a number of nuns that they warned parents against their daughters participating. Padre Bruno would go with some of the group to inform the parents about its activities and dispel their anxiety.

External opposition served only to strengthen the solidarity of the group. Though serious-minded, the group was far from solemn, having a spirited, playful and affectionate character. Appreciative of Padre Bruno's determination to include them, however, the girls were protective of his efforts, and avoided intimate personal relationships with boys in the group. *"We felt that he alone among the congregation of priests believed in women and that he could work with us. So we took care to be super responsible,"* says Graça. Nevertheless some of the girls were forming relationships with boys outside the group. They kept them secret from other nuns and priests but confided in Padre Bruno, discussing with him the experience of being in love and how to relate as a couple. Such was the responsibility of the group that some of its strongest opponents among the nuns became its advocates and the experience doubtless contributed to the school's subsequent decision to become a mixed school.

Weekend activities were planned and reviewed by the group, with Padre Bruno facilitating the participation of all the members. On occasion the girls or youths would decide they wanted to meet separately. If it was the girls, the boys - in a role reversal astonishing at that time - would facilitate, undertaking all the domestic preparations - shopping, cooking, cleaning, preparing the premises. The girls would reciprocate. Following such separate meetings there would invariably be a party allowing the two groups to reintegrate and exchange experiences.

What attracted the young people most to the group was Padre Bruno's faith in their ability to shape their own lives, the strong sense of personal growth and purpose they derived from it and their experience of solidarity. *"It was very unusual for a priest or nun to sit and discuss our problems with us. Generally they would discuss them among themselves and then let us know their decision,"* said Graça. *"But Padre Bruno would tell us that the problems we experienced in life were ours and it was up to us to think them through and find solutions. We would discuss many of these problems with the group. When we decided what action to take, he would encourage us to take it and then examine its effectiveness afterwards."* A group approach to problem solving - discussion, plan of action, action and review - was established at the beginning.

Padre Bruno also entrusted the group members to work as volunteers in the church. *"Most of the priests and nuns were Italian. Padre Bruno is from Italy, too, but he doesn't count - he is completely Brazilian. Anyway, even the volunteers who supported the work of the congregation were brought over from Italy, as if we Brazilians were not up to it. It was a hangover of the colonial period,"* said a group member.

As part of the weekend experiences, members of the youth group worked as animators in the Oratory. A celebratory Salesian Sunday event, the Oratory was open to children and adolescents from the neighbourhood and offered catechism classes, sports, cultural and other recreational activities. The experience helped sensitise the group members to working with poor community children.

The youth group explore their own city

To take their ideas forward, the group embarked on a physical exploration of their own city, visiting wealthy and very poor areas, including their home districts. Their investigation led them to try different kinds of intervention.

Graça remembers becoming aware of a old woman in her own street whom she had seen almost daily. *"She lived in miserable conditions with a sickly daughter and grandchild. The child was malnourished and would play in the filthy water in the open drains. I noticed her after we read of Christ going to help people who were poor and excluded, and I spoke to the group about it. We took some landfill to her house because the plot she lived on was a swamp. After that I started seeing people in a different light."*

Bank personnel manager Rolando Maneschy, who was to have a long association with the youth work, first became aware of the group's activities through the involvement of his own sons. One night they failed to return home. He knew they were with the group and went to look for them in the early hours. He found them working with other young people helping a family reconstruct their shanty home which had collapsed in a storm. *"I had taken part in the church movements before but not stayed with any of them, but this really grabbed my interest,"* recalls Maneschy.

The members of the group would discuss the effectiveness and limitations of their interventions, in what constituted an exploration of the scope for humanitarian action. Their discussions began ranging beyond the bounds of the Salesian College. They would attend meetings with other groups in other areas and from other churches. Every now and again they would encounter a more overtly politicised group, linked to an underground party and subject to security police harassment. *"There was some mutual criticism,"* said Jaime. *"They said politics was about something other than going to mass, holding meetings and doing social work. There was no point in what we were doing. Trying to change the world by good actions would take too long. We also felt that our action had to become more focused."*

The group's conceptual reference at this time was Don Bosco rather than Karl Marx. Don Bosco - founder of the Salesians - dedicated himself to poor children in Turin in the 18th Century. He established a school as a community, emphasising the development of the individual within the community of others. The presence of the educators in the children's lives and the quality of the relationships developed between them were regarded as the bedrock of the educational process. There was also an element of co-responsibility, with older children actively supporting the process and participating in decision making [8].

Some of the Sacramenta group, however, also studied Marx and other socialist thinkers. Graça, for instance, was part of another group that met secretly in the crypt of a church. *"We would hear about the struggles of Fidel Castro and about Che Guevara,"* she recalls. *"There were young people who wanted to break the crosses and said we should go armed against those who held power. Others argued for a pacifist approach."*

Discovering children on the streets

In exploring the city centre, the group found beggars living and sleeping on the streets and started to make regular rounds at night, taking a thermos of coffee, bread and cigarettes and talking with them. In this way they also discovered children on the streets. They were not street children - in the sense of having abandoned, or been abandoned by their families. Such children only began to appear in Belém with the deepening of the economic crisis at the end of the '80s. The public tended to think of children on the streets as thieves but these children were working to help support their families. After several visits, the group identified a concentration of working children in and around the area of the fresh produce and fish markets in Ver-o-Pêso, next to the busy fishing-boat harbour and the commercial centre of the city. They decided to focus on these children because they had their lives ahead of them and more might be done with them.

"To this day," says Jaime, affectionately, *"I don't know if Padre Bruno guided us to this choice, but we ended up dealing with the declared objective of the Salesians. He never told us what we should do but I feel there was a fine conducting thread that led us to this point of arrival."*

The children had various occupations - they sold cheap shopping bags, lemons, parsley and any other small items that might find a buyer. They often went hungry, having no food on setting out from home and no lunch on the street. They would eat sherbet or sweets to keep themselves going. There was a constant pressure on them to earn. Few attended school. They suffered exploitation and other abuse by adults and were constantly tempted

---

[8]For an introduction see *The Salesian Way of Educating, Walking with the Young*. Patrick Laws, Salesian Publishers, Metro Manila 1993

10

to meet their commitments to their families by resorting to petty crime. In opening a dialogue with them, group members also began to visit some of their homes. Most lived far from the centre on peripheral 'invasion land' in shelters that in many cases were no more than a wooden box a few metres square. Many were from broken homes. Often the adults in the families were unemployed or in informal employment. *"We were appalled at their living and working conditions,"* says Georgina, another member of the original group. *"But we also had a naive belief that we could act to change this reality. Later we came to realise it would take more than our action to accomplish that."* For the moment the question was what could they do?

State and church policy for socially abandoned children

Prior to the dictatorship, state social policy was based on the assumption that needy children posed a threat to society. Misdirected and erratic welfare assistance to families was accompanied with harshly punitive treatment of anyone, including children, suspected of straying into criminality. In principle, the National Policy for Minors' Welfare, introduced early on by the military regime, and subsequently the Minor's Code, constituted a shift from a correctional to an assistance model. Children were redefined as being in 'irregular situations', circumstances attributed to parental failure. Policy was formed centrally by the Federal Government through the National Child Welfare Foundation (FUNABEM). It was executed by state-level affiliates of FUNABEM, commonly called FEBEM, but in Belém called FBESP. The FEBEM established referral centres in the state capitals and closed institutions, known as boarding schools. This restructuring, however, inherited the buildings, equipment and personnel, and with them, the repressive institutional culture of the preceding system. The correctional model was never displaced, and welfare practice remained shot through with abuse and corruption[9].

Any child picked up by the police or handed over by a member of the public as being in 'irregular circumstances' was referred to children's judges. Poor children had no legal representation and so the judges became lone arbiters of their fate and, effectively, lone makers of social policy. Committal to the reformatory-style institutions became routine. Many such institutions were isolated and very large - one in Belém was actually located on an island. They constituted little more than warehouses in which the

---

10 Hector Babenco Elenco's film *Pixote* gave the world an indelible insight into the worst of this policy.

nation abandoned its neglected and unwanted children[10]. This out-of-sight policy produced an out-of-mind effect on the population, disrupted only when an adolescent committed some offence, reinforcing public hostility. Few institutions were adequately equipped, or attempted, to prepare the children in their care to assume a role in society.

In time, the system became overwhelmed by the sheer numbers of children. Children were routinely held in adult jails before being sent to 'temporary' screening centres, where they might be kept for lengthy periods waiting to be processed. Many escaped, only to return to the streets and be rearrested. There were cases of children going through this nonsensical cycle more than a hundred times. Eventually, the system became recognised as providing an education in dependency and criminality and as reinforcing a public perception of poor children as bandits and 'marginals'[11], to be feared and further oppressed. It was this perception that underpinned the impunity with which children could be treated, including ultimately, their assassination by 'justice committees' - death squads composed of small businessmen and off-duty police[12].

Another major flaw was that the law failed to distinguish between working, needy, abandoned and criminalised children. Many youngsters fell to the rulings of judges simply because they lived in poverty. Furthermore, the greater number of children who wound up in institutions were placed there not by the authorities but at the request of desperate parents who no longer knew how to control or provide for them.

---

[10]Institutionalising of children in Brazil was started by the Jesuits as a way of hiding illegitimate and unwanted children, including the progeny of masters and slaves, as well as orphans sent out from Portugal. From 1738, circular revolving platforms were constructed in the walls of a number of institutions. An unwanted child could be deposited on the platform which was then given a turn, delivering the child into the institution. Sometimes the corpses of children were deposited in such contraptions. The mortality rate among children in institutions was as high as 40 percent. Benedito Rodrigues dos Santos, an activist intellectual prominent in the struggle for children's rights, associates the practice of institutionalising children with a strongly patriarchal social system and with infanticide. He reports that the last of the circular platforms was dismantled in São Paulo as late as 1940.
[11]People who have been marginalised and come to be regarded as outlaws.
[12]For more on the killing of children see *Brazil: war on children*, by Gilberto Dimenstein, 1991, LAB.

The quest for a different way of working

The youth group learned of the state welfare provisions through the children they met on the streets and through a number of children who, in an agreement with the state, attended the Salesian Occupational School. They also went to visit some state and other institutions. Graça recalls bursting into tears when confronted in one state institution by children of 10-12 years hungry and screaming in prison-like conditions.

The group was clear that streets were no place for children but there were no ready-made alternatives to their being there. What was more, as working children, they were contributors to their families' survival. Taking them out of the street was not an immediate option. Giving them some kind of handout assistance was not sustainable and could well undermine their independence, creating the false expectation that someone would be on hand to solve their problems. It would also fail to tackle the underlying causes that led to their being on the streets in the first place. Crucially for the development of the participation and organisation of children, the group decided to abandon any kind of charitable response and instead set out to form a friendship with the children, to find a way forward with them. *"In doing so, what was uppermost in our minds was not the neediness of these children but their potential and possibilities,"* says Padre Bruno.

Another fundamental idea was that, in forging an alliance with children that society had turned its back on, the members of the youth group would be forming a new and opposing social relationship, from which both would change and learn. But first a way was needed to get to know the children.

At that time, children working in Ver-o-Pêso had difficulty obtaining food. The group sent two of its members to look at a soup kitchen for working children in Recife in the north-east of the country. The decision was then taken to open a Restaurant for Small Vendors near to the market area. At the time this was a very extraordinary idea, one that attracted considerable media attention. The group chose the term restaurant, rather than a canteen or a soup-kitchen, in recognition of the children's status and dignity as earners. A token price was charged for the food.

Chapter two

From restaurant to republic

An abandoned salt storeroom - a stone's throw from the market area - was acquired through the Bishop of Belém. The group set about energetically cleaning it up, making repairs and converting it into a restaurant. A foundation in the city, linked to the Salesians, gave them the equipment and then a cook was hired. The restaurant opened for business on 12th October 1970. Padre Bruno launched a campaign in the church and the community to mobilise supplies of food.

In what was probably the first street-based initiative of its kind in Brazil, group members began to go daily to the streets to contact children and invite them to the restaurant for lunch. They and Padre Bruno made a point of sitting with the children, eating with them when there was sufficient food, doing without when it was short.

Carlinhos, today a trade union activist, was among the first children to attend the restaurant. He recalls his amazement at sitting down to eat with the group members and Padre Bruno. *"Even at home such a thing would never happen,"* he says. *"My father would tell us that he was commander of the family, and so should eat first, and get better food. The rest of us ate what was left."*

The whole venture was new and explorative to all concerned. No-one involved knew where it was leading. In undertaking this new work, the group members began to refer to themselves as volunteers. Since no-one was rewarded to do such work, it could have emerged only through voluntary action.

Building a new pedagogy

The volunteers plunged into their experiment with as much good humour as determination. The first hurdle to overcome was the suspiciousness of the children, who were more accustomed to indifference, mistrust or aggression from adults than consideration. On the day the restaurant opened, a scare was put about by children that the food was poisoned. At the start of the '70s youngsters on the streets of Belém were teenagers, almost exclusively boys. Strangers who approached them usually wanted to exploit them, or were enforcers of the law and city regulations, who wanted to place them in institutions.

Some of the youngsters from the streets were so emotionally deprived that they would struggle against anyone offering affection, testing the authenticity of the offer to the limit. They brought the neglect, violence and rejection of the streets and, sometimes, of their homes into the relationship with the volunteers and into the restaurant. At times they would fight one another, rowdily throw food about or hurl plates to the floor.

The volunteers had to struggle against the impulse to reject the most rejected of the children and to be affirming of them, to displace their own tendency towards indifference with friendship, to exercise authority without being authoritarian. None of this was easy.

"I felt very angry. I was a young woman and they had to obey me," was the initial exasperated reaction of one volunteer to the children's defiance. *"At first we would order aggressive boys out of the restaurant. But Padre Bruno would invite us to understand their aggression and how it was socially reinforced, as well our own reaction to it and to consider the causes. We had to learn patience."*

While the volunteers had gained some experience in working with children from their work in the Oratory, the Salesian Sunday event, they had had no special training and there were no books to tell them what to do in working with children on the streets. Some of them were beginning to study social work or psychology at university. But the teaching of these disciplines lacked any human rights framework. It was so tied to government and professional practice, and to the social process of containment and institutionalisation, so uncritical of the social context and unrelated to social change that it was of little value. The volunteers were explorers of new terrain. Their progress was not linear; it involved numerous diversions, loops, repetitions, losings and regainings of the way. There were im-balances to be corrected. At one stage they thought idealistically that anything the children wanted was right. *"That was a journey to nowhere,"* says Padre Bruno. By trial and error, practice and review they learned to negotiate a more concerned and respectful relationship with the children, demonstrating respect while, at the same time, making it clear that respect has to be a two-way transaction. *"We really want you to be here. But you are here of your own choice and you can also choose to go. If you choose*

16

to stay you must respect the right of others to take part," was the kind of argument they might put to a disruptive youth.

They were helped forward by the children themselves, most of whom warmed to the relationship they were offering and the general conviviality of the restaurant. As they steeped themselves more in the boys' reality, they came to realise that the violence they displayed was imposed on them by their experience and so might yield to different experience, just as some of their own responses to the children were imposed and could be changed. This was no mere theoretical process. There were real grounds to love and respect the children. In the face of public disdain and the dangers of the street, most worked faithfully and even with a sense of mission to help their families survive. Most had engaging and admirable qualities - including a readiness to respond positively to positive approaches, to play and to joke - which survived the highly adverse circumstance of their lives. In time, and in differing degrees, the volunteers worked through the sense of themselves as being superior to the children, or as owners of knowledge and acting benevolently towards them; they gained a real experience of mutual respect, in which both they and the children increased their insight into themselves and into the forces at work in society.

Through the relationship with the children, the volunteers understood more clearly that poverty was no accident but a social product fashioned through the systematic denial of opportunities and resources to an underclass. You could choose to ignore this process of exclusion, or work to change it, or exploit the opportunities it offered for your own advancement. But you could not abandon people to poverty without abandoning something of your own humanity. Marginalisation was not just something done *to* people condemned to lives of poverty, it was something that also happened *inside* them, and *inside* the people whose choices brought about their exclusion. What was marginalised - and might instead be nurtured - was our common humanity.

Companions in crisis

Being with the children in moments of crisis was crucial to winning their confidence and respect. One day some volunteers - all girls still in their mid-to-late-teens - were called by children to help an adolescent in trouble. He was lying on the pavement in a high fever. Graça was among the volunteers. *"We were not very experienced*

17

and didn't know where to go with this boy and he said he was too ashamed to tell anyone what was wrong with him," she recalls. "We urged him to tell us and he pulled his trousers down and showed his penis - which was terribly infected. For us this was a tremendous shock. We took him to the casualty department of the hospital. The treatment was very painful so we stayed holding him for support. It was remarkable experience for the boy because up to that point no-one had been concerned about him. Later, in talking with other children, it came out that he had been sexually abused by women in a brothel. It was a remarkable experience for us. It made us more aware that, though we were poor, we had a lot going for us - family and friends who cared for us, food, clothes."

The group was not always able to help. On another occasion Padre Bruno and two of the volunteers came across a child who had been stabbed by a beggar and was lying unattended in the street. It was an area where taxi-drivers took their cabs to be cleaned by young car-washers. The boy was bleeding to death. Padre Bruno pleaded to the cabbies to take him to hospital but none would help. A youth washing cars promised to clean any cab free of charge which took the boy. Another shrugged and spat and said the boy was good for nothing and should be left to die. Padre Bruno leapt into the traffic to stop passing cars but none would help. He and the volunteers then carried the boy to nearby shelter and called the police. He died several hours later still awaiting their arrival.

Such exposures to public indifference towards a dying child shocked the volunteers to the core. They had to find a way to combat this unconcern. Some kind of campaign was required.

The relationship with Padre Bruno

In finding their way and developing the new skills they needed, the volunteers had as a powerful point of reference the relationship fashioned between themselves and Padre Bruno. Inspired by the ideas of Don Bosco, he was developing both his own and their empowering and facilitating skills. He would stimulate rather than lead discussion, ensuring the participation of all involved. He would encourage the volunteers to refine their ideas and then act on them, resisting the temptation to intervene, even when he believed he had better solutions than they. He then helped them evaluate their experience. They loved the relationship he offered them because it amounted to an act of faith in them and liberated in them a new sense of self.

Padre Bruno is physically small and slight, though straight as an arrow and with a natural authority. His playful disposition is tempered by a steely determination when it comes to the well-being of children and he is described by those who know him well as having great charisma. His view is that everyone has their own charisma. His own he attributes to a deeply held commitment to allow the free flow of ideas.

"He was not like any other priest we knew - he would really listen to us and help us to work out what we thought about things," says Graça. *"In our families we did things because we were told to do them. It was not so much our material poverty that rankled in us, as the accompanying emotional deprivation in our homes. Adults at that time were sombre and closed. Our fathers made us fear them. Our mothers were doormats. Father Bruno showed us we were capable of making our own decisions. He was transparent, in that he would let us see that he also had failings and made mistakes, that he was also a human being in the process of constructing himself. That gave us freedom to expose ourselves and reveal our fragile sides and made us closer to him.*

"I don't know how to explain it to you, but it made us feel stronger - it gave us courage to face everything and go forward. We did things we never did at home with our families. For instance, carrying earth as landfill - but we did them with so much love and strength. We didn't learn any of that from preaching. We felt we wanted to do it out of the love we felt for this relationship with Padre Bruno. He gave us so much more than information. He gave us that too, but he was contrary to all the models of man we had - those men who were never wrong, powerful men, the one that commands, that shouts, that suffocates you. He gave us another model. It was very important."

Just as the volunteers felt they could talk to Padre Bruno about anything, he in turn would orient them to pay similar careful attention to what the least powerful people in the community had to say, specifically the children they worked with.

Making mistakes and feeling free to openly acknowledge them in a dialectical process with others was seen to be crucial to learning and to the group building faith in its ability to find the right way forward. At the same

19

time Padre Bruno was in the background intervening in situations that might be damaging, particularly to the children. He worked with the volunteers both one-to-one and as a group. *"Sometimes he would intervene in a concrete situation - if we responded aggressively to a boy who was trying our patience, snapping at him, for instance, that he would get no lunch that day. Padre Bruno would talk to the child and pat him on the head. The child would calm down and then Padre Bruno would say to the volunteer, 'Let's give him lunch because he is feeling better now.'*

"He would never reject you for something he thought you did wrong. What he did was give you attention. He would say what he thought was wrong and invite us to reflect on the purpose of our work. Were we acting in the best way to achieve it? How could we do it better? He helped us to make the best decisions but we always felt, in the final count, that the decisions were ours.

"The relationship with Padre Bruno was very strong - for many of us he substituted the family. Many of the youth transferred to him the image of father or mother, or the friend or companion they didn't have. We were sure that he was always with us."

The volunteers were also sustained by the strong bonding they were building with each other through the work, through the weekends they spent together and through daily reflection on, and weekly self-evaluations of, what they were achieving.

They would arrive at the restaurant just before midday. After lunch there was a period of games and informal discussion with the children, which in time became more structured. Then at 2.30 p.m. each would go his or her own way. The restaurant itself was represented to the children as a function not of charity but solidarity, its existence made necessary by the injustice of children having to go to the streets to work in the first place. Transparency and collective decision making were key features of the relationship developed within the restaurant. The children were told how the food and other resources were procured and distributed. They were encouraged to participate in the day-to-day decision making. In one discussion, for instance, they agreed in future to clear away and wash their own dishes. In their work with the children, the group began to feel it really was building a different kind of social relationship and, in doing so, proving that such a relationship was possible.

Most of the members of the Sacramenta group look back at their experience in the early stages as one of spiritual awakening. They had a strong sense of reconstructing themselves, releasing and strengthening the humanity in themselves and others and identifying and discarding destructive reactions acquired unconsciously, through the medium of their homes and schools.

For Georgina, at the heart of the experience was an exploration of the meaning of Christianity and of the notion that Christ exists in every person, including the children on the street. The awakening to Christ - or, in secular terms, humanitarian qualities he symbolises - in oneself and others, delivered the possibility of a utopia in which all people had space to move and breathe and where all rights were respected.

For Graça, the spirituality of the experience was nothing to do with the mystical spirituality of conventional church teaching. *"It was something implicit in what we were doing. We were like the groups at the very beginning of the Christian movement, before the successive amendments by the churches over the centuries. What impressed me was the humanity of what we were engaged in, the discovery that it was up to us to take responsibility for nurturing the humanity in ourselves and each other - not an individual humanity but the collective humanity. Even though Padre Bruno also put great effort into creating very beautiful Christian celebrations in the church, that for me was not the fundamental point - the fundamental point was this issue of his humanity. I never really associated him much with the church or the priesthood; much more with this keen awareness that we are in the world and face the challenge of what we are to do about it. I always have fights with Padre Bruno on spiritual issues. But I listened to him when he said if we cannot change ourselves we can change nothing."*

Chapter three

Getting organised: children's work co-operatives

In their discussion with the children, the volunteers drew on the experience they had gained in their own discussions with Padre Bruno. They tried in a non-directive way to encourage them to talk about their lives and the difficulties they faced and to identify possible solutions. *"We made it clear we were not going to solve their problems. We were there in friendship and solidarity and would support them in their efforts,"* says Graça. Here too the volunteers had to work to acquire a new orientation and new skills. *"Just learning to control the impulse to take the lead, to direct the children was a constant learning process for us,"* says Georgina. They had to learn how to engage children in decision-making, not just offer them the opportunity - how to elicit their views and then help them work through their ideas and develop plans for action; how to support them in that action, even at times when they were not convinced it was right course; how to encourage them to review what had been achieved.

Their discussions revealed that, while the children had some problems in common, others were specific to the occupations they followed. This prompted their organisation into co-operative groups based on their street occupations. Each group worked with particular volunteers. The first formed were the *sacoleiros* - who sold imitation leather plastic shopping bags. The volunteers encouraged the boys to plan how the group should operate. Carlinhos was a *sacoleiro*. *"We used to buy ready-made bags from a man who lived near my house. But then we got organised. The volunteers helped us get raw materials. Five of us made bags. Twenty others sold them and then we shared the profits."* The children began to hold regular meetings to discuss any problems that arose and how to overcome them.

Other groups quickly followed - paper bag sellers (*saceiros*), shoe shiners, car washers, newspaper sellers and there was also a miscellaneous group who sold diverse small items, pens, lollipops, sweets. Membership of the groups was not rigid; the children could move from one to another as they switched street occupations.

A new more formalised occupation was opened up when a commercial firm operating hire-purchase agreements expressed an interest in getting children to deliver letters to its customers. The volunteers helped the children to start a messenger service. Georgina, who worked with this group, got to know every corner of the city.

Action taken by the groups

The volunteers worked in shifts to fit in with the demands of the different occupations of the children. Because Padre Bruno had a car, it fell to him to work with the newspaper sellers. Between these children and the publisher of the newspapers was a hierarchy of middlemen, dominated by the chief *baderna* (which literally translates as a *disturbance*). This distribution king would buy the entire issue of the paper and sell it on to a number of lesser *baderneiros* who in turn sold it to stall holders, who then sold to the children. The child's margin was minuscule and if he did not sell all his papers he had no money to buy fresh stock the next day. The volunteers circumvented the *baderna* mafia by arranging to buy papers direct from the publisher. The daily transaction was done at the newspaper office at a rowdy pre-dawn gathering of the chief *baderna* and *baderneiros*. Padre Bruno and other volunteers working with the group would get up at three in the morning to join them, buy the papers and distribute them directly to the children. *"We had a place where we met them and it was a real* baderna,*"* he recalls ruefully. *"At one point we had around 100 children in this group."*

Elimination of the middleman was a concern of a number of the groups. The paper bag sellers *(saceiros),* for instance, turned to manufacturing their own bags from empty cement packets instead of buying them. In doing so they had to find out where to get materials, how to make the bags, how to evaluate the profitability but they also had to decide between themselves how to work together and how to share the profits fairly. The *saceiros,* for instance, decided that each child should take a turn at each aspect of the work and that profits should be shared equally.

The co-operatives as an educational opportunity

The organisation of children into work co-operatives later became practised elsewhere in Brazil and was transferred through international contacts and agencies to other countries. The co-operatives in Belém, however, were never regarded simply functionally, as a means to prepare children for the world of work or to increase their income. First and foremost they were a

24

good way at that particular time in Belém to bring working children together, strengthen their relationship with the volunteers and develop rich educational and developmental opportunities.

Involvement in the co-operatives allowed the children to experience themselves and each other in a new way, and form relationships not easily fashioned amid the unrelieved competition and opportunism of the streets. They acquired new social and practical skills as well as a sense of their own potential. They learned to analyse their circumstances more thoroughly, to argue a case, to identify their problems instead of just reacting to them, and to seek systematically ways to overcome them. The volunteers encouraged them to act on their ideas as a group and then evaluate the results. By working with each other and by tackling common problems together, they built an experience of solidarity - equality, sharing, affection, co-operation.

Conflicts between the boys - whether petty acts of meanness or real aggression - would be picked up and worked through with the volunteers, who would try to get to the bottom of the issues, bring opposed parties together and make peace between them. General issues illustrated by such conflicts - such as other expressions of aggression in the family and community - would be discussed in the groups.

Above all, the affirming and respectful relationship offered by the volunteers and the experience of solidarity gained through the co-operative groups gave the children the basis for critical awareness of the social and economic relationship they experienced in their own families, the streets, schools and community. Why were love and respect so little evident in other contexts? Why did children like themselves have to work on the streets and be excluded from school and other opportunities? Why were their own families and many other people made to live in poverty?

Children on the streets risk a deepening alienation from their families and a disdain for their own social class and cultural heritage. Because of their poverty, their families can offer them little protection and few if any of the opportunities and status symbols of the city. Because breadwinners in their families work long and uncongenial hours and travel miles across the city to work sites, home can as easily be an empty place - physically and emotionally - as well as overcrowded. In talking about their lives, the children were encouraged to be more understanding of their families, who were also exposed to the extreme stresses of poverty, and of the communities they lived in.

All kinds of issues were brought up by the children for group discussion - their sexuality, problems faced by their families, violence directed at some of them in their own homes and in the community. Through discussion and evaluation the rote lessons of their daily experience - which suggest that opportunism, aggression and criminality pay - were converted into a real learning experience, one intended to intercept the reproductive cycle of social violence.

The volunteers realised the value of what they were doing over a period of time. *"It wasn't so clear to us at the beginning. We had a general idea of doing preventative work in the way of Don Bosco. We wanted to help the children to become good men and citizens instead of marginals. We were explorers who progressed with the children by means of action and evaluation. We made a more systematic account of what we were doing only several years later,"* says Georgina.

Children's view of the co-operatives

Nearly a quarter of a century on, people who were children in the first co-operatives speak appreciatively of their experience and praise the affection, the spirited companionability and the playfulness of the volunteers. *"We would leave home full of needs,"* says José Carlos, a former *saceiro*. *"We were children without parents, or whose parents had no space in their lives for children, or who did not know what to give a child; whose parents worked hard and were not educated themselves. For some, the volunteer was father, mother and friend. I don't doubt that I had a most privileged education through the volunteers."*

Former *saceiro* Carlinhos also looks back appreciatively to the relationship with the volunteers: *"I grew in every way. Today I am not an alienated person. I have insight into the way society works. I am critically aware. I question everything and I am teaching my daughters to do the same."* Today a trade union activist, he and his fellow former *sacoleiros* still meet annually. Others among them have taken up leadership roles within the popular movement in the State of Pará and they still consult each other when they face problems.

Another boy at that time, João Gomes, is now a prominent leader within the community association movement in Belém. He started selling lollipops on the streets at the age of seven in the inland town

26

of Castanhal. His mother brought him and his brothers and sisters to the Sacramenta district of Belém after separating from their alcoholic father. She got a very poorly paid job cooking for nuns. João Gomes was introduced by another working child to the Restaurant of Small Vendors. He joined the Messengers Group run by Georgina. *"We delivered letters by bicycle. We were given a lot of human warmth by the volunteers and we felt we were really valued,"* he recalls. *"It was also very good to be in a group - to be learning new things, discussing, taking part, voting. And we had excursions to the country. It was all very exciting, because it helped me understand my situation as a member of a suffering class. Of course that was a process. At first not many things caught my attention - I just wanted to play. But I really liked being with the others in the group. I liked the discussions."*

Children march to the City Hall

The international frontier between the rich and poor worlds, which runs across national boundaries and through towns and countryside, is patrolled with varying intensity by ubiquitous men in uniform - soldiers, police, security guards, as the case may have it - and, in some more ragged parts of the frontier, by un-uniformed death squads. Generally, the well-to-do barely notice this army of defenders; it is the poor and dissatisfied who get to stare down their gun barrels or feel the weight of their batons. In Third World environments, the guardians of the more contented realms of society are themselves generally poorly trained, underpaid, usually armed and recruited, as a crowning cynicism, from the same pile of disposable humanity they are paid to keep at bay.

Children ensuring their families' survival through their work in the streets are no less subject than others to the harassment, exploitation and, not infrequently, brutality of the guardians of 'public security'.

One face of this officialdom in Belém is the *rapa,* or municipal police force, which has the Canute-like function of trying to deter unlicensed hawkers flooding the city streets and threatening the equanimity of the comfortably-off. The children are not entirely innocent. One of the few amusements open to them is ducking and diving from the *rapa,* though its consequences can be far from amusing.

A new way of working with the children was foreshadowed in an incident that occurred in the second year of the Restaurant of Small Vendors existence. A municipal inspector had found a child bag seller asleep on the pavement in the commercial area during the lunch period, when businesses close. He confiscated the boy's merchandise. A large group of boys gathered and, armed with sticks and stones, advanced on a bar where the man was drinking. On the way they encountered Padre Bruno and some of the volunteers and explained what had happened. After some discussion it was decided that they should go and talk to the man.

"There was a crowd watching all this and, instead of an attack, it turned into our first demonstration," says Padre Bruno. *"We spoke to the official on the children's behalf. He protested that he was just following orders. We then all marched to his official headquarters and negotiated an agreement that the children would be left to trade unmolested. In reviewing the incident with the children, we agreed that instead of trying to attack the police and officials we should get organised in future to press for better working conditions."*

Struggles against the *rapa* resurfaced periodically following a defeat. The *rapa* would lie low for a while only to re-emerge refreshed to the task. In another incident, some time later, children and adult traders from Ver-o-Pêso marched on the City Hall. The *rapa* had again seized merchandise without issuing receipts. Some children who had lost their wares had retaliated by throwing stones. They were beaten and arrested. At the mayor's office the marchers demanded their release and the return of their merchandise, their working capital.

Among the demonstrators was José Carlos of the *saceiros* group. *"The market was like a big family in those days - everyone knew everyone and this demonstration happened spontaneously. The* rapa *was the common enemy. If anyone spotted the* rapa *he would warn the others. I sold bags and sometimes tomatoes. We all had little trays to display our goods. We would put these trays on crates. If the cry went up* 'rapa!', *we'd snatch up our trays and disappear. Anyway after they'd caught us this time someone shouted: 'Lets go and get our merchandise back!' Others cried, 'I want back what is mine,' and 'I want my capital back'."*

"They didn't let us into the City Hall, but the mayor summoned the head of the rapa. *We were many and had a lot of witnesses to the seizure of goods. The mayor ended up listening to us. He ordered the release of the children and return of the merchandise. It was very rare for us to get our*

merchandise back. So it was a real victory. There were no volunteers with us but we told them all about it. They said it was great; that was exactly how to do it."

Living in community

The new direction of the work was making increasing demands on the time of Padre Bruno and the volunteers, most of whom, like the children, had to make long journeys to and from the centre every day. Padre Bruno sought permission from the congregation to withdraw from the Oratory and move, with six of the volunteers, into empty rooms above the restaurant. Though highly unconventional, his request was granted.

Young women volunteers were not able to sleep on the new premises, but every effort was made to include them as fully as possible and, for their part, they were determined not to be left out. *"We would arrive at the crack of dawn and leave at the last possible moment late at night, so as to miss nothing,"* said Georgina. The very fact of a priest living with youth had drawn unwelcome speculative comments, and the girls realised that a mixed residential community would at this stage have been a bridge too far.

"In those days anything of any importance was decided at meetings of men," says Graça. *"If women tried to join in they would be mocked as hunting for husbands. The important thing about our group was that we were participating in all the discussions and played a full part in the decision making."*

Those who took part remember the experience as joyful and enlivening and speak of the deep sense of camaraderie they developed. Serious in his commitments, Padre Bruno has a keen appreciation of jokes and pranks. One volunteer recalls returning unwarily to the restaurant on a sweltering Belém afternoon to have a bucket of cool water tipped over him from an upstairs window. Glancing up, he glimpsed Padre Bruno ducking back out of sight. *"He was always ready for a pillow fight or throwing foam when we were washing up. Sometimes we all went away together - the movement had a friend who owned some islands in the river and we would stay on one. We would go crab fishing. One day someone hung a crab on Padre Bruno's shorts and he raced around trying to get away from it!"* recalls José Carlos.

"It always gives me great pleasure to meet friends from that time," recalls Jaime. *"When we woke we would have a moment of reflection before*

breakfast. Then we would all go our different ways. We would meet again at night, cook a meal together, tell jokes, talk, listen to music. Sometimes a group of us would go off to the movies." At the weekends the volunteers would go back to their homes to see their parents and get supplies of clean clothing. They had open access to Padre Bruno. *"He gave up a lot of his usual religious routine to be with us,"* says Jaime.

By this time, all the volunteers in the core group were from poor backgrounds - others having moved away to take up other opportunities. Most of those who remained - some 20 in all - continued to work or study in part of the day, but a number were now working with the children full time. Padre Bruno was worried that as a priest, with a congregation to rely on, he enjoyed a higher degree of security than they. Concerned about their future, he urged them to become employees of the restaurant. There would be some way to raise the money. Receiving some payment, he argued, need not detract from their voluntary motivation.

"He was thinking about our pensions and the number of registered working years we would accumulate with the Welfare Ministry. But it was only two or three years later that I agreed to having a signed work contract," recalls Georgina. *"It was so rich and rewarding a time we gave ourselves totally to this work. We agreed to accept only expenses. We did that only because we had family expectations to contend with - we had studied and were foregoing a job in a bank or something because of this involvement. We were known as full-time volunteers."*

Padre Bruno would go to the homes of the full-time volunteers to explain their activities more thoroughly to their parents, most of whom then began to support rather than oppose their children's participation.

Chapter four

A Republic of Small Vendors

Things were way down the road from running a restaurant. A new name was needed. But what was this new experience being developed by the volunteers and children about? At the heart of it was the effort to build loving and respectful social relationships in which all involved were encouraged to have a say. The key features were those of a thoroughgoing participative democracy. Accordingly, in 1971, the Restaurant of the Small Vendors changed its name to the Republic of Small Vendors.

In the context of a military dictatorship which ruthlessly suppressed its opponents and showed no sign of coming to an end, the declaration of a republic, particularly one that generated some demonstrative action against the local authorities, might have been less daring than foolhardy had there not been well considered ambiguity in the choice of name. Organisations of university students in Brazil are also known as republics.

"If university students, then why not street children? However, for us on the inside the political connotation was what mattered. It was revolutionary," says Graça. *"We were engaged in a conscious exercise of participation. The structures we created, the relationships we fostered within our Republic were an implicit rejection of the state's denial of that right."*

There was another reason the Republic had little to fear from the state security services. *"Children were regarded as being of no political significance, least of all children on the streets. They were considered to be the business of priests and women,"* says Padre Bruno.

Developing democratic practice

In addition to work-group meetings, the Republic began to hold assemblies to decide on matters of general interest, such as problems with the *rapa*, or to elect work-group co-ordinators from among the volunteers. Those elected composed the Council of the Republic. The assemblies served to broaden the children's interests out from their own immediate work groups. Rolando Maneschy, the bank personnel manager who became interested in the work of the youth group through his sons' involvement, recalls very well attending

31

his first such assembly. He had retired from his job and told Padre Bruno he wished to make himself useful in any way he could, but he did not just want to be an occasional supporter on the outside, he wanted to be directly involved.

"Of course, the work was intended to be an experience for youth and children, not for adults like me. So my application had to be debated," he recalls. *"The children were electing group co-ordinators. Then they went on to discuss whether I should be allowed to work with them or not, and in what way! It was a very strange experience for a former personnel manager. I just sat and listened. I will never forget it and have always respected it. They finally deliberated that I could play a part as a supporter and adviser, but I wouldn't be able to hold a position or vote. I accepted at once and worked with them for the next 16 years."* [1]

Taking the work forward

The volunteers began to work in other ways to open up new possibilities for the children. They began to seek the support of adults in the children's lives. They spoke to market stallholders in an effort to promote more positive attitudes towards the children. Wherever possible, they made contact with the children's families. Just as they encouraged the children to reflect on the struggle of their parents, they encouraged parents to be more conscious of the contribution and needs of their children and to think of ways of easing the burden borne by the children. Often just having the interest of an outsider made parents more aware. The volunteers were particularly concerned that children should not be deprived of an education by their need to work.

Families had various attitudes to schooling. A good number could not afford to keep their children in school though they would have liked to. Some parents were demoralised to the point where they had become active exploiters of their own children and had no interest in their schooling. Many, lacking any formal education themselves, had little grasp of its value. Yet others compromised, sending one or more of their children out to work so that their siblings might continue at school.

While the volunteers encouraged parents to place or keep their children in

---

[1] Though far from wealthy Maneschy and his wife concern themselves with the problems of people in poverty in other ways; for instance an elderly person joins the family every day for breakfast and another for supper.

school, they began to learn that the problem of non-attendance lay less with the families than with the glaring inadequacies of the schooling system. Schooling was simply not available in many cases, especially in new invasion areas. Where schools existed, they were just not geared to the reality of the lives of children from the 'invasion' districts. There was no recognition that such children were already breadwinners with important family obligations or that they struggled across town to get to school and would arrive tired and hungry and sometimes late. Instead of working in a committed way to integrate children regarded as a problem, the schooling system tended - as it sometimes appears to do with disaffected children in Britain today - to insist that they conform and, when that failed, to discourage actively or exclude them from attending.

The volunteers tried working with schools to get them to accept children and with the children to support them in their attendance, but their efforts were complicated by a conflict between the educational experience offered by the Republic and that available in school.

Wherever the values fostered by the volunteers engaged with the prevailing value system, there were contradictions and ambiguities to be dealt with. In their co-operatives, the youngsters were encouraged to question and participate. In school, such behaviour was regarded as impudent or disobedient.

José Carlos was among the children in the Republic who also attended school. *"I used to be very shy at school, but after being involved in the groups I began to protest. People thought me very strange,"* he recalls. *"For instance I was working during the day and studying at night. I had a teacher who, if he missed a class during the week, would demand we attend on Saturday. I began to say, 'No, I came on time during the week. On Saturday I've got to work.'"* At that time few protests against the system were heard. *"It was the dictatorship, we had to learn what they wanted to teach us and do what they told us to."* It was easier for children to drop out of school than change the system.

Such contradictions were always discussed in the groups, helping the children develop critical awareness of the society.around They also made it clear that stratagems were needed to survive the system without capitulating.

33

Trying to penetrate the work market

Work aimed at strengthening the autonomy of the children had to start from where they were - on the streets and squares and in the peripheral zones of the city - but it also had to help them go forward from there. Street work supported the family but did little to equip children for the adult world of work. Opportunities were needed for them to move out of the streets, if and when they chose, which would also take account of their families' dependency on their earnings.

To try to open up formal employment opportunities, the volunteers started an Employment Agency. The messengers' co-operative, with its more structured work demands, provided a valuable staging post for adolescents making the transition from the relative indiscipline and playfulness of the street life for the discipline of a job.

The Employment Agency brought the volunteers right up against the rejecting periphery of established society. Few employers would even consider taking on adolescents with a street background. Of those who would, most were looking for cheap labour. They offered informal work, often in dangerous or unhealthy conditions. Very few employers offered opportunities likely to be beneficial to the adolescents - providing proper training, according them workers' rights, allowing them time to continue with their schooling. Prominent among those who did were adults who had consulted Padre Bruno about leading a Christian life.

The Employment Agency would refer children to jobs that seemed half promising and then try to negotiate employees' rights for them. If they failed they might then cancel the contract. Because the children were fully consulted, the quest for employment also provided them with a new perspective on society. José Carlos was one of the first to be placed in work by the agency. *"We took the work even though the employer refused to sign our documents or pay us overtime,"* he says. *"We were eight boys working in the timber shop doing the work of adults. The machinery was unguarded and very dangerous and we worked an eleven-hour day. I lived far away and had to get up at five in the morning. On leaving work I went straight to school in the evening. I got home at about 11 at night."*

The volunteers tried to negotiate better employment conditions. When they failed, José Carlos left the job and returned to the streets. A year later he got a placement with another company, as an office boy. This time he was given proper training as an electrician, and subsequently as a driver and store keeper. *"I was very lucky,"* he said.

The Campaign of Emmaus

The idea of youth from poor districts working voluntarily with children on the street was something completely new and it attracted considerable and generally favourable local publicity. The work was commonly mis-represented as charitable and, given the context of the dictatorship, the Republic was not moved to explain its activities in any depth.

Publicity served a number of purposes. There was no point in directly confronting a dictatorship or in attempting to influence its policies or practices, particularly as they were formulated centrally at a great distance from Belém. The Republic did want, however, by demonstrating a different and better way of doing things, to expose the violence and bankruptcy of state provision for children from the social periphery. To this end Padre Bruno and the volunteers also kept well clear of the state. They sought no official permission for their activities, declined offers of state funding and avoided any association with FUNABEM, the federal department responsible for children 'in irregular circumstances' or its agencies. Meanwhile they regarded strong public support of their work as a hedge against potential state intervention.

Publicity was also essential if the Republic was to influence public attitudes towards children from poor communities. For some time it had talked of launching a sustained campaign to raise both funds and public awareness, but lacked the skills and hours in the day to take the idea forward.

The matter of funding was of growing urgency as the work expanded. Ad hoc donations of food were no longer adequate for operating the restaurant. The Republic was no keener to seek funding from international development aid agencies than from the military regime. They would also try to influence its evolution. They would demand time-consuming reporting procedures and the setting of targets in what was an essentially open-ended exploratory process. Such concerns aside, the more interesting route was to encourage the citizens of Belém to engage with the problems of their city.

In some of the Republic's deliberations, Padre Bruno had made a practice of calling on people with expertise - teachers, psychologists, social workers, media people and others. He wanted to tap their knowledge but it was also a

35

way of mobilising wider concern about what was a socially engendered problem. Favourable publicity gained by the Republic enhanced its ability to call on middle-class professionals who were influential in Belém. Finally, a group of people, some associated with the church and others outside it, asked to become involved in a more concerted way.

The work with children itself was reserved for young volunteers. But the new adult support group could help in other ways. Padre Bruno called a meeting of the group at which it undertook to plan and help execute a city-wide campaign. Its members, among them people in key positions in the media, took up the idea with great enthusiasm. It was to be called the Campaign of Emmaus.

Why Emmaus? *"After Jesus' tomb was found to be empty, two close friends of his were walking along the road to Emmaus when they were joined by another traveller,"* explains Georgina. *"On arriving at the town, they decided to eat together. By the manner in which the stranger blessed and broke the bread to share it, the men recognised him as Christ. Emmaus is the place at which the resurrection of Christ is witnessed."* With an imaginativeness characteristic of the popular movement in Brazil, the campaign encapsulates two powerful ideas - the moment of awakening to Christ who accompanies us unrecognised in the children of the streets, and the sharing of resources.

The support group designed and planned the campaign over four months in close consultation with Padre Bruno and volunteers. The first campaign was heralded by a sequence of enigmatic advertisements simply announcing over a two-month period, **"Emmaus is coming. Wait!"** Many people thought Emmaus was a new product. Leading advertising agencies in the city were involved and, in following years, took it in turns to promote the annual event without charge.

Invitations went out through the media and were delivered door to door inviting people to donate goods for which they no longer had a use. Businesses and corporations loaned lorries, drivers and petrol during the week-long event. Hundreds of young volunteers were recruited from schools, universities and church groups. Their job was to go out with the lorries to collect the donations. Materials for banners, food for campaign volunteers - everything was donated. The first campaign was held in May 1972 and was, literally, an overwhelming success. The glut of donated goods delivered to the Salesian School choked the classrooms and corridors.

Classes had to be cancelled for a week. *"To free the building we quickly sold what was saleable and had to burn the rest on a huge bonfire,"* says one volunteer.

Apart from the professionalism with which the campaign was planned and publicised, other elements contributed to its success. It was a very surprising event; nothing like it had been done before. The cause - to support youth from peripheral areas of the city who volunteered to work with the children of the streets - was also astonishing and wonderful. Then, it was a rare opportunity during the political oppression for people to exercise their citizenship - to get involved, take the initiative and assume some responsibility for something happening in their own city. Furthermore, the campaign carefully avoided becoming an instrument of political or commercial patronage masquerading as philanthropy. Whether you gave a notebook or house (as one woman did) donations were anonymous.

Finally the physical nature of the event was highly appealing. Cash donations were neither sought nor accepted. The campaign enabled the city to gain a sense of itself, albeit fleeting and tenuous, as a community pulling together - a glimpse of its own humanity. More than 20 years after the first campaign, the young volunteers who take part in these collections today speak of them great enthusiasm.

The campaign appeal was not to people's charitable inclination but to their willingness to share. Donated goods were sold cheaply to people in poor areas of the city, rather than to maximise profits. Those who bought them were represented, not as beneficiaries, but as also contributing to the work with children on the streets. The values sought symbolically in the campaign were solidarity and redistribution.

The volunteers hoped the campaign might eventually become a demonstration of the city's solidarity with poor community children. They hoped to see donors graduate from disposing of items they really did not want to giving up resources that mattered to them, in the same spirit as they devoted their time to the work.

They settled for a strategic approach, however, and did not initially share these ideas fully even with the support group. The first target was to build up public trust in the work before using the campaign in a more concerted way educationally. In the event, donations reflected the full spectrum of possible responses - from people taking the opportunity to rid themselves of junk to spirited acts of solidarity. There were cases of children giving their own bicycles and even their own shoes to the passing campaign lorries. In succeeding years the campaign message became more demanding until a phrase which encapsulated the essential idea was arrived at - **"Solidarity for transformation"**. This was retained as the core message of the campaign which nevertheless continues to address different themes each year.

"We could see that in the campaign we had real potential to sensitise people in Belém to the plight of children in the city and to mobilise them. We felt our work might even become an expression of the people of the city," says Padre Bruno. *"In the event we didn't realise everything we hoped for but we did become respected, even loved, by the city and that greatly increased our ability to influence events."*

"We tapped people's good will, but I don't think we moved many people to the point where, if they saw something bad happening to a child, they would intervene in solidarity with that child," reflects Georgina.

More than ten years after this early social mobilisation approach to development was pioneered in Belém, it was to be applied at a national level and then propagated internationally as a development tool by UNICEF Brazil.

One unforeseen bonus of the campaign was that it was to assure the Republic of a sustained supply of new volunteers. It became the main means of attracting new young recruits.

Within three years of the forming of the youth group, great strides had been made. A totally innovative way of working with children on the city streets had been initiated, from which all involved derived a strong sense of motivation and personal development. The Republic had established its right to operate independently of the authorities. It had established the principle of engaging its own city in what it was doing rather than turning to international funding agencies. It had won significant support from members of the public and developed a means both to raise funds and mobilise further support. And it had achieved all this through the voluntary action of its members and supporters.

Chapter five

The development of the Republic

In the minds of those involved, the Republic was not a place or an institution. It was a culture or a movement - a way of being in the world and relating to others. In fact the culture incorporated a deep mistrust of institutions and the tendency of the latter, from the state down, to subject human lives to institutional needs. As a member of the Republic put it: *"People are not in the world to serve institutions. It should be the other way about."* A new physical location was also needed, however, to cope with the annual influx of materials from the Campaign of Emmaus, a need reinforced by the unexpected loss of the property that housed the Restaurant of Small Vendors.

Within the Salesian community, the work had admirers and detractors. Critics felt that it was too political or unconventional. Although the congregation freed Padre Bruno to engage in it, the overall attitude was more one of toleration rather than endorsement. At that time, the Bishop - later to become one of the Republic's greatest benefactors - could not even bring himself to speak to those involved in it. He withdrew the property, complaining that the Republic had never paid the rent and the premises were needed for other purposes.

The support group who had helped with the campaign again proved its worth - offering to purchase land. A large plot was found, the size of four football pitches in what was then a very poor neighbourhood, some three kilometres from the city centre. Used as Military Police stables, it was little better than a swamp; a canal running through it flooded periodically. There were no habitable buildings and so a simple house on stilts was constructed in a corner of the plot.

By this time some of the original youth group had moved on. Among them, Graça had left to study at university. Jaime was soon to follow. The rest of the group and Padre Bruno moved to the new house. Before the plot could be developed there was a massive job of landfill to be done. Luckily, a major site was being excavated for the construction of the City Market and the soil was dumped on the new property free of charge.

Other buildings were needed, including a warehouse for the Campaign of Emmaus, a meeting room and a kitchen. Under Salesian regulations no building could be started until the cash to complete the job was in hand.

Again the Republic turned, not to external funders, but to the people of Belém, mobilising their support, rather than cash, through the media and the schools. Its headquarters were constructed by means of a massive *mutirão* (community effort), involving hundreds of people. Members of the Republic and of other youth groups visited schools. They asked primary school children to donate a brick each. In high schools, they asked each class for a bag of cement. More that 50,000 bricks and 700 bags of cement were given.

Contractors contributed equipment, transport and expertise. Entrepreneurs provided arches for the warehouse roof. All kinds of volunteers, youth, people from the immediate neighbourhood and children of the Republic contributed their labour at weekends, with professionals and skilled artisans directing the activity. *"There was mud everywhere,"* recalls a volunteer. *"We were well and truly in the mud." "Many people helped build the Republic. Everybody wanted to be involved,"* says Maneschy.

Unexpected interest was shown by a large disreputable mongrel which attached itself to any group that was going. *"Whenever two or more people got together, he would suddenly be there,"* recalls one of the volunteers, *"so we called him Comunitário (Community)."* When a visiting priest brought an Alsatian with him that fought Comunitário, the volunteers took the hound for his own safety to the outskirts of the city and dumped him. But he was soon back. *"There was no getting rid of Comunitário,"* said one. *"Our joke was that, however far we took him, he would just follow the nearest street child straight back to us."*

Bridging the gap

The restaurant had been ideally located, in the city centre where there was a concentration of working children. It was part of their space. Ways now had to be found to link the children to the new headquarters.

The volunteers began to spend part of the day in the Ver-o-Pêso market area and part in the headquarters. Each day the children would be transported to the Republic for lunch, recreation, and group activities associated with their co-operatives. About 100 children were involved. Eventually the Republic obtained an old bus to convey them. Though not ideal, the situation was workable while there were relatively few children. Working children from the immediate neighbourhood also began to take part. Saturdays were set aside for recreational activities, with other children of the local community joining in.

At the new headquarters there was plenty of space to play - a great liberation for children confined to neighbourhoods of narrow lanes and small, tightly packed dwellings and often mistrustful adults. Games were a feature of activities every day. Football and volleyball pitches were prepared and, over the years, a rich variety of socialising games was elaborated by the volunteers. *"We wanted the Republic to be a place where the children could also have fun, especially in playful activities that build relationships,"* says Padre Bruno. *"Games can give people the chance to get to know each other and agree rules, and they also allow for spontaneity."*

Most of the children on the streets of Belém were from Indian migrant families from the interior, or black families, the descendants of slaves, who have moved to Belém from the north-east. Their self-esteem was undermined by their low social status, the poverty they lived in and the daily challenge of city values to those of their own cultures. Even so, the north of Brazil is rich in traditional games, dances and events, with many celebrations crowded into the month of June. From the outset, the Republic had made a point of encouraging the children to learn about and celebrate their cultural traditions to reinforce their sense of social identity. Now it could enter more fully into the spirit of these activities. The children were able to prepare costumes and learn dances such as the *carimbo,* typical of Pará and *capoeira,* the dance-form of a martial art brought from the African continent by slaves and once banned by the colonial authorities. They participated in such events as St. John's Party festivals, marked by traditional food, dancing and public ceremony. Every Sunday there was the Oratory, the Salesian event, for children from the Republic and its neighbourhood.

All but one of the children's work co-operatives were still operating. The plastic bag makers (*sacoleiros*) had been defeated by a lack of working capital and inflation. With prices spiralling upwards, middlemen had bulk-bought plastic and other materials and so could undercut the price for which the children could make the bags. Another casualty - some time later - was the messengers' co-operative. It was closed down by command of the Post Office, a monopoly which would not tolerate even the children's small encroachment on its territory. Each of these defeats was discussed with the children, the learning value fully extracted, giving them deeper insight into the society they lived in. In time the newspaper group was also to collapse, due partly to the organisational inexperience of the volunteers working with the group at that time.

Jobs in the bank

The Republic's Employment Agency had at first tried to place children with smaller employers, including doctors and lawyers. A problem was that most were offering only full-time employment, however, which would prevent the children from attending school. A breakthrough came with the negotiation of an agreement with the federal bank, *Caixa Economica*.

Here Rolando Maneschy's banking experience was put to good effect, although he doesn't claim the idea to have been his. *"It probably came up at a meeting of a support group. Padre Bruno invariably invites the opinions and help of other people when there is a problem. So you will suddenly have a meeting of ten people or so of diverse professional experience. The solutions to many problems have been achieved in that way,"* says Maneschy. Maneschy, however, took the proposal to the bank's board of directors that they offer adolescents formal work experience. They liked it but wanted to take it over. The Republic insisted on managing the project; it wanted the work to go to children from the neediest of families who were under most pressure to go to the streets to work.

The Republic proposed an employment agreement based on discussions with both children and parents. It stipulated a four-hour working day and formal employment conditions. For their part, candidates had to agree to continue with their schooling and contribute their earnings to the support of their families.

The Republic got much of what it wanted but failed to get permanent employment status for the children. Initially, it also had to settle for half a minimum wage for what was half a day's work[1]. The agreement provided, and continues to provide, 70 openings for adolescents of 14 years of age who have attained a certain educational level. Technically the Republic is the employer

---

[1] This sounds reasonable enough but the value of the minimum wage was severely eroded by inflation.

but the bank pays the wages. The contract ends when the young workers turn 18, though the bank may offer some of them permanent posts.

Following the bank agreement, the Employment Agency changed its name to the Formal Work Market. The agreement is typical of the kind of bargain the Republic strikes in the socio-economic environment in which it has to operate. Inevitably, there is compromise but a compromise that meets several crucial needs of the children and their families - income, formal work experience and educational guarantees.

Some years later, other programmes for poor community children negotiated employment agreements with banks and other corporations, though in many cases the terms were less favourable. Padre Bruno campaigned unsuccessfully to get them to form a united front in negotiating better terms and also tried without success to persuade the federal bank to make the Belém deal available nationally. Other banks have initiated employment opportunities for adolescents, but the work has gone to the children of the staff rather than street or working children.

The Employees' Group

As usual, the Republic's aim in developing its Formal Work Market was not just to improve the employment chances of some children lucky enough to get on to the scheme. In preparatory discussions, parents strongly endorsed the idea that the opportunity should be developed both for its employment training value and as a means for children to learn about the world of work, including workers' struggle for their rights.

To achieve this wider educational purpose, an Employees' Group was formed. The group met at the Republic on Saturdays. Discussion about immediate work problems provided the basis for the wider exploration of related issues - employment practice, work conditions, the accumulation of capital by owners and shareholders, workers' rights and responsibilities and the role of trades unions. Conflicts between the values promoted within the Republic and the workplace would also be explored. For instance, adolescents who showed an interest in employees' rights might be less likely to get selected for permanent employment. Discussion of this issue and how to deal with it, might lead to a more general discussion of employers' resistance to workers' organisation.

Although children in the Formal Work Market scheme were from the neediest families, the Employees' Group was bigger than other groups in the Republic; its members wore distinctive bank uniforms on work days and had met certain educational requirements. For these reasons there was a tendency among them towards elitist attitudes. Typically of the Republic, this negative outcome became an educational opportunity. *"Some in the Employees' Group began to complain that they didn't want to share the restaurant with children dirty from the fish market and other street occupations. We had to do a lot of work to counter this tendency for them to disown their own origins and we were helped in this by the children who were leaders in the different groups,"* says Georgina. *"We would reflect with them on how such attitudes mirrored society's rejection of street children and its tendency to denigrate them collectively as pickpockets and thieves."*

General recreational activities for all children in the Republic were also held on Saturday and provided an opportunity to bring together children in the Employees' Group and those from Ver-o-Pêso, helping to dismantle the tendency towards elitism.

From bank worker to activist

Members of the Employees' Group generally speak favourably of the attitudes towards them of the bank staff and heads of departments. João Gomes remembers their friendliness. They even held collections to give him Christmas presents. But the work was also his first exposure to middle class life-styles.

At a time when he wanted to attract girl friends, he felt very frustrated that he couldn't afford the stylish clothes and shoes of some of the regular staff. He gave part of his wages to his family but with what he kept for himself he got into a phase of drinking more than was good for him.

He went from the bank on to other jobs and involved himself in struggles for workers' rights. In a factory, he became active in a co-opted union which held no membership meetings and whose president was close to the employer. He helped initiate discussions with a small group of activists about the state of the union, poor pay and dangerous working conditions. They began to mobilise the workers in the factory and to hold regular union meetings. Worker participation in the union began to strengthen but, after organising a major assembly, João Gomes was sacked. Now a prominent local leader in the popular movement, he says ruefully: *"I wasn't too strong on tactics in those days."*

Expressions of the Movement

With the launch of the Formal Work Market, the number of children involved in the Republic grew rapidly to about 150. At the same time the annual Campaign of Emmaus was becoming a major annual event in Belém. In its peak years, it mobilised more than 800 lorries and drivers loaned by businessmen and 1,500 young volunteers. Sorting, valuing and renovating the donated goods was growing into a massive recycling undertaking. Staff had to be employed and managed.

Each year a Campaign theme had to be chosen and its promotion, through professional advertising, door-to-door pamphleting, the press and public meetings, including debates in community centres in poor districts, had to be co-ordinated. Themes have included violence against children, the rights of children, the working child, the child and the family and many others. To this day, the Campaign retains enthusiastic media support, both from journalists and advertising agencies who continue to give their services free of charge.

Preparation of each year's intake of campaign volunteers gave the Republic a singular opportunity to get its messages over to members of successive generations. Celebratory gatherings were held at the Republic to explain what the big donation was about, why it was needed at all and how the struggle of children on the streets was part of the wider social struggle of people excluded from mainstream society. The demands of the Campaign on the volunteers was threatening the quality of their work with the children and it was decided to establish a separate co-ordinating committee of volunteers.

The Campaign and the Republic were referred to as 'experiences' rather than projects, reflecting a mistrust of institutions and of becoming institutionalised. As the notion took root of their being autonomous but interrelated parts of a movement they came to be referred to as 'expressions' of the movement[2]. Even today, those involved in the movement will tell you that none of the activities or institutions of the movement are so sacred that they cannot be changed to meet the changing demands of the times.

The Republic and the Campaign were bridged by an annual assembly, in which the children also took part. At this assembly the past year's activities were reviewed and evaluated and future priorities and policies decided. Among other issues, the assembly decided on pay levels for staff. Initially it adopted the principle of payment according to needs. One result was that the cook at the time, who had several children, was being paid more than the co-ordinators of the sections.

First steps towards training

The Republic needed periodically to replenish its volunteers. In fact, few people could take the arduousness of street work for more than two or three years. Some of the volunteers undertaking university social work courses had tried recruiting fellow students; this proved unsatisfactory as the latter tended to treat the experience as an adjunct to their studies and to vanish during the holidays. Happily, the Campaign assured that there was a continuous supply of new volunteers but did little to prepare them for the work.

The apprenticeship with Padre Bruno that the pioneers of the movement had undergone was not a practical basis for preparing successive waves of volunteers. The Republic established a small training centre, with the training at first undertaken by Padre Bruno and experienced volunteers who stayed on with the movement. It also appointed a social worker and later a psychologist to support the volunteers who felt out of their depth in dealing with families with chronic problems such as child abuse. These professionals, however, also had to be trained in the values and methodology of the Republic before they could be really effective. The introduction of training made it necessary for the Republic to define more clearly the educational principles inherent in its work.

---

[2]More 'expressions' were to manifest themselves. For the sake of coherence this text will refer to them either individually by name or collectively as the Movement of the Republic from now on.

Republic on the move

In the latter half of the '70s, Padre Bruno accepted new roles within the church which strengthened his ability to mobilise support for the new approach to working with poor community youth and children. He became director of the Pastorate of Youth in the diocese and subsequently Secretary of the National Council of Brazilian Bishops for the Northern region. *"I ended up knowing everyone, everywhere,"* he says.

A fortuitous meeting in Belém with Edmund Kaiser of the Swiss agency, *Terre des Hommes,* based in Lausanne, took the movement into a new phase. The Republic had a reputation for turning down international aid agency funding. In fact, what it wanted of such agencies was the kind of relationship it was striving for in Belém - based not on charity, or aid, but solidarity. Solidarity, however, was not generally on offer. On the contrary, the charitable appeals of international funding agencies to their donors cast the latter as benefactors and so fudged the relationship between the comfortably-off and the poor. *Terre des Hommes* was an exception. Kaiser said that in his travels he would act as an ambassador for the work of the Republic. Even so negotiations with the agency went on for nearly a year and a half. The final arrangement provided the Republic with core funding over a good number of years.

The argument advanced by *Terre des Hommes* for the acceptance of its funding was that it would enable the movement to expand its work to reach 450 children. *"It's not that we were being tempted to try solving the problem of all the children on the streets of Belém - we never had illusions about that,"* says Padre Bruno. *"Such solutions aren't possible without major changes in public attitudes and in economic and social policy. Our objective was to work for those changes by developing and revealing the potential of the children and demonstrating the injustice of their being on the streets. People were by now making favourable comparisons between our work and that of the state, so one aim was being realised. However, the number of children on the streets was growing and we felt we could not shirk our responsibility to them."* Not only was the number of children increasing, reflecting a deepening crisis in poor families, but there were more hawkers generally competing for a living, rendering the street environment more hostile.

Work with street children in other parts of the country

An important development in the latter half of the '70s was that a number of organisations were beginning to develop work with children on the streets in other cities and came to see the work of the Republic. A member of the Minor's Pastorate, which was establishing street level programmes in Sâo Paulo, spent 15 days in the Republic. The Pastorate had been created by the National Conference of Brazilian Bishops (CNBB) in 1978. It developed an assistance programme for street children, helping to pioneer the role of street educators[3], and became active in many parishes in different parts of the country.

Padre Ramiro, who became well known for his work with children in Recife, capital of the State of Pernambuco, stayed in the Republic for three months before launching his programme in Jaboatao. Other visitors were Salesians from Belo Horizonte who were starting occupational training for adolescents. Because of the high cost of travel in so immense a country, however, and because the organisations working with children had no wish to attract the attention of the authorities, there was little ongoing communication between them.

Getting big and getting lost

The *Terre des Hommes* funding enabled the Republic to recruit rapidly new paid volunteers, resulting in a sudden influx of people who were inadequately prepared. The number grew to 50, but the quality of their commitment and aptitude was patchy. Among the newcomers were what the core group began to identify as 'party volunteers' who were there principally to have a good time, meet each other and hang out at the weekend. Street-level work became neglected and lost its continuity as the volunteers drifted into the easier course of relying on children coming to the headquarters. The same investment was not being made in the relationship with each child or between the children in the groups. *"We were slipping into a mass production mode,"* as one volunteer put it, *"something we were highly critical of in state practice."* In addition to the influx of new volunteers, the number of paid support staff in the Republic also increased, among them people who simply wanted a job.

Among the new volunteers in this phase was Inácia Souza, who is still with the Republic today. Like many others, she had first become involved through the Campaign. *"It was a very difficult moment,"* she says. *"People were despondent. We felt overwhelmed by difficulties. It seemed we didn't have the right motivation any more."*

---

[3]A role similar to that of the volunteers in the Republic.

Chapter six

Getting better organised: the emergence of grassroots nuclei

An emergency general assembly was called to discuss the deteriorating relationships with the Republic of Small Vendors. *"We did something very surprising. We decided that the way out of the crisis was to stop everything and for all of us who worked directly with children to go back to the streets and relocate ourselves in the children's reality,"* says Inácia.

A pilot group of the most committed and experienced volunteers was selected to lead the return to the streets. Among them, Georgina established contact with car washers in Avenue President Vargas. She talked with them about their lives and went to visit some of their homes in swampland far from the city centre. She told them about the work of the Republic, encouraging them to find out more about it. Padre Bruno began to work with newspaper sellers close to the Republic. Lucia Gomes, who had joined the Republic at the end of the '70s and was involved in the black women's movement, tried to follow up on children in a notorious and violent red light district.

By going back to the streets, the educators reaffirmed as a priority the quality of the relationships they formed with the children and each other. They also adjusted the power balance in their relationship with the children. *"We inverted the roles that we had drifted into,"* says Georgina. *"Instead of waiting for the children to visit us in the Republic, where they were the visitors and we were the owners of the space, we went to the streets where they were the occupants and we the visitors."* One of the educators, walking in the closed commercial centre of the city at night recalls being warned by a young girl, barely into her teens, *"You shouldn't be here at this time. It's very dangerous."*

After a few weeks, the pilot group reported back for their work to be evaluated by the general assembly. In this way, their legitimacy to evaluate the work of the others was established.

The rest of the volunteers were then given several weeks to develop their own work with children before reporting back to the evaluation committee. They went as individuals, not as members of the Republic. *"What we were evaluating was the degree of commitment and ability of each of us to engage in the world of children in the street. It was a personal immersion in the reality of the children - not an institutional one,"* says Padre Bruno. *"Each person devised his or her own experience in the street - some for the first time."*

A few never reported back, while others came to recognise that they were not suited to the work. Of a complement of 50 volunteers at the beginning of the shake-out, 20 remained to rebuild the work of the Republic.

In evaluating the result of the return to the streets, the Republic found that most of the volunteers had become involved with a particular group of children which met regularly. Some of these groups were based, as in the past, on street occupations, while others had a different basis, such as a shared neighbourhood or locality, in some cases in the invasion areas. At a time when organisations in other centres were just beginning to discover and respond to street children, the Republic's concept of its constituency broadened dramatically. *"We didn't have to restrict our attention to children working in the city centre. We could foster the participation and organisation of poor community children generally on whatever basis was valid for them,"* says Padre Bruno. With this change the Republic began to refer to the groups of children it worked with as *nucleos do base* (grassroots nuclei[1]).

"We were ready to respond to children who spent time on the street, whether they were working or simply had nowhere else to go and whether they were in the city centre or in their own communities," says Georgina. *"We started again with around 20 groups of children. The demand was enormous. Our only limitation was the number of committed volunteers we could muster and the time they had available. Some studied at night and so were unable to meet children who could meet only at night. Soon we were working with twice the number of children envisaged when we first accepted the Terre des Hommes funding. We had grassroots nuclei in just about every part of the city."*

---

[1] This technical phrase is more accessible in Brazil than in the UK. The idea of nuclei which seek to expand their influence in the community around them is common currency in the labour movement and the Workers' Party of Brazil. The *base* refers to the broad social base of the oppressed who support the smaller middle class and the tiny pinnacle of the elite in the representation of society as a pyramid.

Attempt to replicate the work

The Republic attempted to extend its work not by expanding its own operation but by encouraging church youth groups in other districts of the city to work with children. Restaurants, similar in function and purpose to the original, were started by new groups in Sâo Brás, near the city bus terminal, and Ver-o-Pêso. Three other points of intervention were established, one operating out of a church in a district called Pedreira, another close to street markets in Sacramenta, where the original group had started, and the third, near to the Republic's headquarters. The hope was that these initiatives would be autonomous. In fact the preparation of the youth groups was inadequate and they failed to progress independently. Instead their restaurants became extensions of the Republic, each being developed by a group of volunteers, including some new recruits from the youth groups.

Building community experience

Few organisations have the courage or insight to admit that they are badly off course, let alone stop operations, abandon newly adopted targets and start again from a more trusted point of engagement. The movement was able to take such action because a core group of people committed to the process were becoming clearer about their aims and methodology. They knew that the heart of their work lay in neither the structures they created nor social theory, but in the quality of the relationships they were able to engender. This principle both challenges and is constantly besieged by the dominant social ethos in which relationships are routinely sacrificed to goals set by individual and institutional power holders and in which people of no service to the power holders are regarded redundant and ultimately disposable.

Within the Republic the process by which goals are achieved is as important as the goals themselves. One might say that the process - that of affirming and celebrating the value of human beings - is the goal, but it is not always easy for those involved to see what is happening. Given the successive through-flow of generations of volunteers and children, the Republic inevitably undergoes peaks and troughs of clarity and accomplishment. What protected it from the trough that followed this start of the *Terre des Hommes* funding, was the continuity of the core group, reinforced by their experience of living together in community.

All along there had been community experiences of varying duration - a weekend, a month, three months, six months - but by now a number of people,

51

among them Georgina and Padre Bruno but also some more recent arrivals like Inácia - were living at the headquarters of the Republic more or less permanently, while others joined them from time to time.

People who took part in these community experiments remember them with great enthusiasm and affection. They also regard them as having had a major formative impact on their personal development. José Carlos, the former *saceiro*, took part in three- and six-month experiences. Although he had had other employment, he had never really left the Republic, having worked at different times as a volunteer or an employee. *"The best moments were when we were together,"* he recalls. *"It gave us a notion of sharing and being available to each other. Some of us worked in the Republic, others in outside jobs. But we shared everything, including all the tasks. We had a box where we put our money - those who had money. Those who didn't, didn't. We took from the box as we needed it."*

What José Carlos valued most was the egalitarian nature of the community experiences. *"Though I was a former street boy, I was treated exactly the same as everyone else,"* he says. *"I felt respected in every way. And I was able to relate directly to Padre Bruno, the person I love most in the world, in a regular way as a friend. Normally, it would be impossible to be on equal terms with a priest - we have rooted in our culture such a terrible awe of priests. But we all got to know each other very well and the relationships in the group became more affectionate, looser, warmer. At weekends we would meditate and reflect together on how to solve problems - usually other people's problems. Sometimes children joined in the community experiences.*

"We were all changed by these community experiences, children and volunteers. I am sure that, as a result, I behave very differently in my own family now than I would have. The community gave me something I lacked in my own home. My mother always worked too hard for us to be close to her. Now, in my own family, I always talk things through. I never hit my children. I trust my wife - it's she who controls the purse strings."

From street child to community activist

João Gomes is another former street child who speaks affirmingly of the community experience. After he completed his time with the federal bank and left the Employees' Group, he was invited by the Republic to become a volunteer. He received some training as an educator and plunged enthusiastically into following up a group of shoe-shiners from Barreiro, one of the poorest parts of the city. *"I went to their homes. It was very interesting. Not that I had any answers. I would just listen to them talking about their lives. These were families living under bridges and in other very bad situations. Some parents would complain about their children and beat them up and want to take money from them. And the children would start spending more time in the streets. At the time I was a child on the streets, very few of us went in for thieving but the social crisis was deepening and these children were already into drugs and petty crime. I saw myself in all of them and really wanted them to understand the proposal of the Republic - particularly the solidarity and commitment to the struggle for justice. I really wanted to help them as I had been helped."*

At the time João Gomes was completing high school, studying at night. *"I would get back to the community in the Republic at eleven. There was Padre Bruno and Georgina and, at the time, Padre Bernardo. We would talk about everything together. Padre Bernardo had a critical analysis of capitalism and its consequences and shared it with us. I would sit and talk with him late into the night - we studied the Tupamarros guerrillas in the Uruguay region, the experience of the Brazilian Communist Party (PCdoB), the situation in the south of Pará where 100 of our comrades were massacred[2]. We studied a book by a woman leader of the miners in Bolivia, Domitila Barrios[3]. I discovered books and started to read everything I could get my hands on! It was a very utopian, socialist, good experience."*

Padre Bernardo was one of a number of priests and nuns who came at different times to work in the Republic and keep Padre Bruno company, because as a Salesian he was forbidden to live outside the community of other Salesians. *"Padre Bernardo was a student of dialectical materialism,"* says Graça. *"So some groups had a chance to learn from him. Both he and Padre Bruno wanted to achieve a more just society, more solidarity. But the basis of*

---

[2] Pará has a bloody history of land struggles with killings of landless peasants.

[3] Domitila Barrios de Chungara, a leader of women in the struggles of Bolivian tin miners, wrote a testimony of her experience, *Let me speak*, published in English in 1978 by Stage 1, London.

socialism for Padre Bruno is Christian love. The ecclesiastical aspect is always present, whereas Padre Bernardo was more overtly political. Whether you can attain socialism without first achieving transformation of thought and behaviour is a matter for debate." Others who participated in the community experiences, Jaime for instance, also speak of the special bond they feel with those who took part. *"I always experience great pleasure when I meet them,"* he says.

Part of the popular movement

Towards the end of the '70s a change began to take place in the political climate in Brazil that became identified as the 'opening-up period' which would finally bring an end to the dictatorship. It was evident that Brazil's economic miracle, much heralded in the West, was a fraud, secured on the basis of disastrous international indebtedness, government control of wages and the exclusion of millions of Brazilians from any benefit. Public disaffection was growing and popular organisation was no longer confined to the shelter of the church. At the forefront of this process were the unions which were being transformed under the leadership of Luis Inacio da Silva (Lula) into a formidable new political force. In 1978-79 Lula led waves of strikes in the industrial heartland of São Paulo and in 1980 the new trade union leaders formed the Workers' Party (PT) which three years later was to mobilise the country in demanding direct presidential elections by 1985[4].

In 1978 in Belém a seminar, symptomatic of the new mood in the country, was held by progressive groups allied to the popular struggle for social change. The Republic took part and for the first time spoke unguardedly about its work in stimulating the participation and organisation of poor community children. *"There was an incredible reaction - it was a revelation,"* recalls Padre Bruno. It was also the beginning of a more concerted effort by the Republic to place working children on the agenda of the popular movement and gain recognition of them as an integral part of the struggle for social transformation.

Beyond wanting the children to become aware of themselves as citizens and as part of the dispossessed working class, the movement hoped they would

---

[4]In fact, despite the return to civilian rule in 1985, the first free presidential elections were held only in 1989, when Lula himself stood for but failed narrowly to gain the presidency, which went instead to Fernando Collor de Mello. (See *Brazil - Carnival of the Oppressed, Lula and the Brazilian Worker's Party,* by Sue Branford and Bernardo Kucinski, LAB 1995.)

contribute to a more general consciousness of citizenship within that class. *"Power ought to be wielded in the service of the population, whereas the dominant ideology ordains that people are treated as objects in the service of the powerful,"* says Padre Bruno. *"A population that has always been educated to be submissive and question nothing, struggles to become aware of the rights and responsibilities of citizenship. To change that, we have to build a new mentality through which the oppressed can become aware of the conditions of their lives and abandon the submissive state of mind. Such awareness is best cultivated early in the human growing process, not in adulthood, but in childhood.*

"We must engage the child in an educational process through which he or she can experience solidarity and equality and develop a consciousness of being the subject of rights. These values are first experienced in interpersonal relationships. Awareness that you are the subject of rights, enables you to see others in the same light, and with that comes the recognition that you have a duty to respect the rights of others, both in interpersonal relationships and in relation to society at large. Such change is constructed over time through new experience and access to information rather than through adherence to dogma."

But if children are to contribute to a more general raising of awareness they have to become accepted as, and recognise themselves to be, part of the rejected or disposable class and to be recognised by that class - the class of working people. *"Identification with the oppressed class enables children to become aware that their oppression is not their, or their families' fault but something imposed on them from without,"* says Padre Bruno. Such identification is hard to achieve, however, the main barrier being that within the class there are gradations of exclusion. *"Workers are not always aware of the processes of exclusion of their fellows,"* says Padre Bruno. *"First World workers for instance have understood little of the exclusion of Third World workers and the latter have not been aware of the exclusion processes affecting child workers, or women and cultural minorities. The working child, who is not integrated into the organisation of workers, is the most excluded of all.*

"How to achieve their integration is another issue. I would say today this is theoretical and will be achieved through a pedagogy of everyday life. It is a very slow and complex process that encompasses the development of the children's self-esteem and self confidence, a discovery of reality in all its contradictory aspects."

In '79 there were May Day demonstrations by organised labour. Children from the Republic who worked on the streets joined in and even delivered addresses. Many events later, members of the Republic cannot recall the content of their speeches but they know they spoke of their own experience with a spontaneity and in a manner less burdened by slogans than other speeches of the day. From then on the children became regular participants in, and speakers at, the May 1st celebrations in Belém. It was a step towards their integration into the struggle of working people and towards their recognising that they were part of the world of working people.

Defining the educational principles

By now the Republic was also clearer about its pedagogy and methodology, which reflect ideas of Paulo Freire and Don Bosco. To summarise key features:

- The educator is not the owner and dispenser of knowledge, but sharer, a facilitator, a companion;
- Within the companionship which educators offer, they cultivate respect, love, affection, acceptance, solidarity - values diametrically opposed to those that bring about the disempowerment and social rejection of a large segment of the human family;
- The children are active participants in their own learning and development, not passive recipients of ideas and values;
- The aim is to offer children experience of themselves as individual members of and contributors to the human community instead of being isolated survivors on the periphery of that community;
- In constructing this experience of community, both educator and child are learners and undergo transformation. The educator enters into a life experience with the dispossessed child in which there is a simultaneous exploration of the oppressive reality in which both child and educator are trapped and from which they seek a way out;
- The educators' authority derives from the fact that they have a wider frame of reference than the children and access to additional information and use both in ways that the children experience as valuable;
- Both the participation and organisation of children are essential components of the process, organisation allowing the child to explore the potential of political action and recognise the importance of building a wider set of relationships;
- The experience of a different social relationship creates the possibility that such relationships might obtain in society at large.

"We had come to understand that no educational experience is politically neutral. It either fosters acceptance of the status quo or it can aim to bring about change. To do the latter, it must raise children's consciousness of reality and, through their organisation, enable them to act to change reality," says Padre Bruno.

The basic material of this new educational approach is the stuff of the child's and the educator's own lives. The starting place is the life-experience of the child on the street corner, or in the market, or poor community. Progress is achieved through the development of playful affirming relationships and active exploration of this environment, its possibilities and limitations. Children explore together as a group supported by the educator. They are helped to define the problems they face in common with each other, identifying possible solutions, taking action and reviewing the outcome. The exploration broadens out from the child's immediate circumstances, to those of the group, to their community and to the location of that community in society. New information is made available through the educators and by visits to different social environments - rich and poor parts of the city, polluted and unspoiled natural environments and so on - and through experimental action and a review of the results, such as the various actions taken against the *rapa* or trying to help others in the community.

The aims of the process are to defeat those influences that promote a psychology of submission and to give children a firm sense of identity and belonging, a heightened awareness of their own ability to interpret their lives, take action and learn from that action, a strong sense of their own rights and responsibilities and those of others, and a critical disposition.

The religiously minded of the volunteers regard themselves as working for the realisation of the kingdom of God on earth, others as building socialism. Even though the utopian dream may never be realised it must never be abandoned, they say, because striving for it informs human behaviour, contributing to a better quality of life and creating ground for hope.

Though the movement works in a political way and actively encourages children to be politically aware and make political choices, it does not prescribe party allegiances. It has always carefully avoided manipulation of its activities by politicians, even friendly ones. In the post-dictatorship years, a congressman concerned about social issues offered the children of the Republic T-shirts bearing his image ahead of an election. The Republic's response was that it was prepared to accept the shirts for use when the election had come and gone.

Similarly, despite its Catholic origins, the movement has never been prescriptive as to people's faith. It takes the liberation theology route of validating individuals' own faiths instead of proselytising. Among both volunteers and children there are non-believers and adherents to different faiths. There is little display of religious icons and Padre Bruno's clothes do not distinguish him as a priest. In the simple wooden house he lives in, on the bank of a heavily polluted waterway, there is a crucifix but on the walls of the room you first enter are also two photographs, both gifts, offering striking images of the struggle against oppression. One is of a man - a fellow priest among the leaders of a demonstration of small farmers - being struck by an armed policeman, blocking their way. The other is of Sandinista fighters boarding a transport plane.

Intensifying the training of volunteers

Volunteers were recruited mainly through the Campaign of Emmaus but also from youth engaged in social activities in the parishes. After every campaign, young people wanting a greater involvement would be invited to training meetings. Towards the end of the '70s, when a new generation of volunteers was recruited, the theoretical dimension of the training was strengthened - a development that again illustrated the Republic's ability to draw on support at key moments from people with appropriate skills. Stella Menezes, of the social work department of the University of Belém, had become interested in the Republic while supervising her students' extension work there. She had worked during the '70s in poor community groups aimed at developing leadership and building community solidarity. She introduced a more structured exploration of the thought of Paulo Freire and other progressive educational philosophers.

The new volunteers were from the outskirts of the city - if anything from more deprived backgrounds than their predecessors - and most had received poor schooling. Some were at first resistant to reading, anticipating that it might undermine rather than reinforce their self-confidence. *"They were more into practice than theory and didn't want to stop and be made to think in a theoretical way about what they were doing. They would have welcomed a practical guide to working with street children but there was no such book. Paulo Freire's ideas were obviously relevant to them but the text had to be made more accessible,"* says Stella Menezes. In fact it was both stimulating and reassuring for the volunteers to discover that there was a theoretical framework for the practice they were already embarked upon.

Training was an adjunct to the Republic's traditional method of enabling volunteers to build their knowledge through the dialectic of trial and error, reinforced by frequent group evaluation meetings. *"The relationship between volunteer and child is vulnerable to all kinds of manipulation and emotional blackmail,"* says Stella. *"The volunteers have to learn how to reveal the game - to say to the child, 'If you scream and throw filth at the walls just to tell me you are here, you don't need to. I know you are here. And I am here for you.'*

"During training we would consider different attitudes towards children. If a volunteer tends to regard children charitably and sentimentally - as poor little things - it can interfere with his or her ability to set limits and creates opportunities for manipulation. In transgressing undefined limits, a child might evoke a punishing response. A volunteer might scream back - 'You'll get no lunch today!' Well, these children were all too used to being screamed at and they had very loud voices. The idea that you could make them obey you by screaming was an illusion. There were other confusions to work through, for instance the idea that you might control a child by denying him lunch. That was not a way to set a limit. It was denial of a basic necessity. Then, if I proposed telling a child who was behaving disruptively, 'If you are not quite ready to do this now, then you are free to go and come back when do want to do it', a volunteer might protest, 'You mustn't exclude this child.' I would explain that this was not exclusion. It was making it very clear to the child that freedom does not extend to disrupting others in the group from getting on with their activities."

The volunteers also had to learn to recognise ambiguities in the early phases of their relationship with the children. *"At first the children might see in me a girl friend, a potential sexual partner, a mother, or a provider,"* says one of the volunteers. In developing the relationship, they had to learn how to show affection in ways that made it clear to the children that what was on offer was a reliable and affirming friendship.

The nature of grassroots nuclei

The forming of a grassroots nucleus takes place over a period of time in which volunteers and children undergo a lively process of self-development. The volunteers are reconstructing themselves as people who do not just wring their hands in anguish at social injustice but take responsibility and act as citizens. The children are developing a sense of competence, self-worth, respect for others, and solidarity with each other - ultimately an experience of themselves as citizens with rights and responsibilities.

But how is this transformation assessed? *"It is easy to see the reproduction of the prevailing value system in the behaviour of children on the streets,"* says Maria dos Reis, who worked as a volunteer in the Republic in the mid-1980s. *"For instance, they act in a very competitive and opportunistic way. Even when they begin to meet in a group, discuss things and take action together, at certain testing moments they will cheat each other. They will push in front of a friend to snap up a sale, failing to recognise that the friend also needs to take money home. If one of them finds a cheaper source for items to sell - bags, for instance - he might fail to tell the others. Of course we reflect constantly on such behaviour in the groups.*

"It's difficult to measure the maturing and strengthening of solidarity but it is easy to perceive it when you are facilitating the process of reflection. A group, whose members were mainly looking to their own self-interest, becomes a nucleus and begins to look at the world and their own behaviour in a critical way. The strengthening of the bonds between the children produces a critical consciousness of the world beyond their group. It is an educational process."

Time and resources have been too limited to allow for a systematic follow-up of all ex-members of the Republic. Some are known to have gone on to become activists and grassroots leaders in the popular movement. *"Not knowing what happens to children after they leave us is one of our big failures. Our great hope is that they do get involved in the struggle for a more sharing society and we certainly know of a number who have,"* says Padre Bruno.

Georgina believes that most children benefit in some way. *"Even children who are not able to overcome the external pressures on them to resort to criminality acquire something of value,"* she says, recalling a boy she visited in prison. *"He urged me to tell other children in the Republic of his experience as a warning not to follow his example. Such feedback is very reassuring, because there are times when we wonder if we are simply pursuing an ideal we can never make real."*

It is when the members of a nucleus achieve their greatest sense of solidarity that they have usually arrived at the end of the process and are ready, as young adults, to take the experience with them on into other activities. Many of the volunteers also disperse into other occupations. Unlike other movements, the movement of children is continuously recreating itself, resulting in successive highs and lows of achievement. *"We are always beginning again"*, is a common observation within the Republic. Fortunately, amid the ebb and flow of its membership, a number of volunteers has stayed on, or returned after a period away, and a small number of children has become volunteers or employees, contributing to a safety thread of continuity.

Consequences of the organisation of children

In time, the idea of grassroots nuclei became a key concept in the organisation of children throughout Brazil. Within the movement in Belém, the development of nuclei had a number of important consequences during the '80s. For one thing, they provided a broader organisational principle than that of children's street occupations. Nuclei can be established wherever children congregate, and on whatever basis may serve - it may be a common occupation but may equally be a common problem, involvement, or locality, such as a given street, or a market place. At different periods throughout the '80s, the organisation of children in Ver-o-Pêso was based less on the work they did than on the violence they met with from adults, including the police, and between themselves.

The new approach to the organisation of children also allowed for greater experimentation in involving their families. The Republic had always been conscious of the fact that children came directly within its influence for only a few hours during a day in which they were otherwise exposed to quite contrary experiences. It had always believed it could be more effective if their families were collaborators in the process.

Among parents living in poverty, many struggle to gain minimal control over any aspect of their lives, including the welfare of their children. In the battle to survive, some become active exploiters or abusers of their own children. Many more are forced to make bitter choices for their children to secure their families' survival. An extreme example, provided by the anthropologist Nancy Scheper-Hughes, is of mothers forced to discriminate between those of their children who are more likely and those who are unlikely to survive. They concentrate their attention on the children they regard as fighters at the expense of the weak, effectively helping determine which of their children will and will not survive the socially created circumstances in which they are forced to live[5]. People who work with abandoned children cite other examples of desperate parents giving up or abandoning a child, to save him or her from the life circumstances they must endure[6], or of sacrificing the best interest of one child to save those of the others. Yet another and by far the more common option is to make children prematurely contributors to family survival by sending them out to work, but to do so involves a loss of control and introduces its own tensions. There is the danger that under pressure to bring money into the home the child will drift into criminality or prostitution, or fall into 'bad' company and abandon the home. The desperation of some parents to keep their children on the straight and narrow has prompted them to hand them over to the police, known for their brutality, to 'knock some sense into them'. Doubtless, some other parents, faced with their inability to protect their children, bow to their fate. Conversely, interest taken in a child by an organisation such as the Republic, and altered behaviour in the child, can kindle in parents a reappraisal and a renewed commitment to the child's education and personal development.

When the Republic's main point of contact was the city centre, consistent work with families was hard to sustain. Most working children had arduous journeys from the periphery of the city to the centre. Furthermore the time they spent in travel, combined with their schooling and work obligations, ate into the amount of time they could spend in the activities of the Republic. Where grassroots nuclei were located in the children's own community and where parents understood and collaborated with the Republic the benefits to the child could be doubled. There have been nuclei that met in the parents' homes, with families totally involved and taking it in turn to host the meetings.

---

[5]As always there is a spectrum of responses - at the one extreme being the withdrawal of parental protection of children in what is a deadly socially constituted environment. In a Brazil study Scheper-Hughes argues that mothers reinvest in children if their perceptions of the child's survival chances changes (*Child Survival*, Scheper-Hughes ed.; *Child Abuse and the Unconscious in American Popular Culture* by Nancy Scheper-Hughes, Reidel B.V. Uitgery, 1987).

[6]As mentioned earlier, most children in state institutions were placed there by parents too poor to take care of them.

A new emphasis on leadership and co-responsibility

With the grassroots nuclei came the idea of working more intensively with the children who were leaders, giving them more structured involvement in the Republic and somewhat reducing the dependence of the groups on particular volunteers. Each nucleus elected a leader and a secretary. The nature of the leadership reflected that provided by the volunteers and Padre Bruno - with the leader as facilitator of the participation of all the individual members of each group.

The idea of co-responsibility for the Republic of the group leaders with the volunteers was also strengthened, deepening their sense of participation and prompting some of them to do voluntary work for the movement in addition to their involvement with their groups. The new arrangement meant that two or three volunteers could work together with a number of groups and their elected representatives, reaching nearly double the number of children envisaged at the start of the *Terre des Hommes* funding.

"We were no longer evaluating our work independently of the children - it was now done together with them," recalls animator Lucia Gomes. *"In consequence we had to inform them more thoroughly about difficulties of the Republic in responding to their needs. For instance, if they said it was necessary to totally reorganise the physical structure of the Republic, we would have to tell them we had limitations, particularly financial limitations, and explain them. If they said they needed more volunteers to follow them up on the streets, we would discuss all the issues with them. For instance, the fact that there was not an endless supply of volunteers to do that kind of work. Were we to employ people for eight hours a day, instead of part time, we would have to pay them more. That didn't mean we volunteers were only working for money but we also had to survive and the work was far more demanding and the hours far longer than ordinary work. We had to explain to them why more volunteers were needed in some districts than others. We would also tell them how important it was that they helped the volunteers in various ways, becoming contributors to the work."* They assisted in the restaurants, in organising recreational activities and in the implementation of an attendance register that was experimented with for a while.

The leaders would report back the outcome of their dialogue with the volunteers to their groups, explaining why some of their demands and recommendations were met and others not. Over time demands of the children in relation to the running of the Republic became more realistic. *"As a group of children gained a better grasp of the spirit of the Republic so their level of participation and co-operation grew,"* says Maria dos Reis.

One indicator of this development was that children would go ahead with their meetings and formulate proposals even when a volunteer was unable to attend. Another was that children were demanding greater accountability of the volunteers.

Lucia Gomes was at first surprised and angered when the members of her nucleus announced they wanted to evaluate her work with them. *"I can't remember the incident that sparked it off - it was something I was responsible for and hadn't done. At first I felt very angry to be told by children that I was doing something wrong. It had never happened to me before. I couldn't speak at first. Then they said, 'Look we are not doing this to hurt you or make you feel bad, we are trying to help make the work go better. You are part of a group in which everyone contributes to decisions. If we feel you are not acting as a volunteer ought to, can't we say so?' "* When she got the better of her irritation, Lucia realised the incident indicated that the work was realising some of its important goals.

One day the elected leaders of the nuclei took organisation a step further by arranging to meet each other. This led to the holding of mini-assemblies and the introduction of a general assembly of the children which began to formulate proposals and choose representatives to participate in an annual policy making assembly of the movement. Previously anyone from the movement could attend the policy-making assembly and exercise a vote, but the numbers of people involved had outgrown this approach. Instead the assembly was composed of representatives from the different branches, or 'expressions' of the work - at this stage the Campaign of Emmaus and the Republic - including, from the latter, representatives of the children. *"With this structure, we for the first time began to get children who were openly critical of the Republic itself, so we knew we were getting somewhere,"* says Padre Bruno.

In another development, the grassroots nuclei gained the right to choose candidates from their groups for the work opportunities made available through the Republic's Formal Work Market. The degree of family need, assessed by the educators, remained a priority in the selection of candidates.

"Being selected was a process; the educators went first to the homes of candidates and discussed the families' needs and the work situation. All of that was considered by the group in making its choice," says Nazaré Costa, who was elected by her nuclei to work in the federal bank.

A new condition was that successful candidates remained active members of their nuclei and reported back to them. The measure further countered the tendency towards elitism in the Employees' Group.

At about this time, the full-time volunteers began to be referred to as animators, emphasising their relationship with the children, rather than their personal motivation. The term 'volunteer' became reserved for adolescents within the movement and others who undertook part-time voluntary work for it. Though the animators were now paid modest salaries, the demands of the work still required of them a strongly volunteering spirit. Some, like Georgina, so valued the idea of voluntary action that they continued to work on a purely voluntary basis - spending part of their day with the Republic and earning their living elsewhere.

Opening up new work options - establishment of the POA

An early demand from the nuclei was for work training for children who could not meet the educational requirements of Formal Work Market. According to Lucia Gomes, the first prompt came from a group of car washers who wanted to set up a service centre. There were insufficient resources for this idea. Instead, some of the group who had worked in a bakery suggested they instead try their hand at making bread and asked the Campaign of Emmaus for a stove. *"It was a good example of children themselves, motivated by the animators, setting about finding the means to implement an idea they had come up with. They got the stove, established their co-operative in a community centre and found an adult in the area who was prepared to help get them going."*

Following this initiative, another group discussed work options and asked the Republic to help establish an occupational training workshop in their own district. An attempt was made to operate a series of satellite repair workshops in poor communities - repairing both goods donated to the Campaign of Emmaus and others brought in by local residents - but it failed. Instead, a training centre, the POA (Occupational Training for Self-Employment), was established at the headquarters of the Republic. Electrical engineer Leopoldo Corrado, a teacher in mechanical engineering at the Salesian Occupational

School, moved to the Republic to help set it up. Over the years, the POA has provided a variety of courses aimed at helping its students to earn a living as self-employed workers. Such employment is thought to be well suited to young people whose street experience ill fits them for the constraints and disciplines of formal employment.

POA courses have included typing, upholstery, wicker work, repair of domestic electrical goods, repair of gas and electric stoves, refrigeration, repair of electric motors, house wiring and others. The repair courses given by the POA recycle electrical and other goods donated to the Campaign.

The courses are free and vary in length from three months to two years. Some are held in the morning, others in the afternoon, at times compatible with the children's various work and school schedules.

The POA is staffed by both paid instructors and animators. They establish contact with the families, going to visit the children in their homes and involving the Republic's social worker where there are difficulties. *"We do everything we can to keep the children in the course and to get them back if they drop out and we also do everything to ensure they continue with their regular schooling,"* said an instructor. Profits from the sale of goods repaired by the children are retained by them, helping alleviate family pressure for them to go to the streets to earn. POA students also eat in the Republic's restaurant.

As with the street work, the POA is not presented as something done for the children but created with them in solidarity in the absence of any provision by society or the state. They help keep the premises clean and tend the garden. Through twice-yearly assemblies of the POA, they have a direct say in how it is run and what courses are offered. At each assembly, the preceding period is evaluated and forward planning undertaken.

Like all the buildings of the Republic, the POA is a basic but effective structure - representing the kind of environment that children will be likely to work in as adults and the kind of equipment they might have access to. But its simplicity also reflects the Republic's investment in relationships rather than institutional development. Some members of the Republic are critical of the fact that many church institutions which set out to respond to people living in poverty over-invest in bricks and mortar and, with the shifting geographic distribution of poverty, often end up as schools for the rich. *"Perhaps we should adopt a more nomadic approach to our work so we can move with the poor,"* comments Padre Bruno.

The courses offered by the POA differ radically from conventional occupational training. In the Republic the aim of equipping the child to become a survivor in the work market falls within the broader aim of stimulating qualities of citizenship - participation, organisation and the development of a critical consciousness. Without such a framework, occupational training for poor community children, which often trails the march of technological development, can all too easily simply prepare them for jobs which do not exist or to be survivors at the expense of others, replicating the system that excludes the poor. Some of the most dangerous and exploitative work environments are to be found in small marginal businesses.

The development of citizenship is realised through the relationship offered by the tutors and animators, as well as through the children's participation in democratic structures of the POA and the Republic and their active involvement in policy making and evaluations procedures. Special 'formation' classes are also held every second week in which issues the children want to talk about are explored - such as sexuality, poverty, the family, relationships with each other and violence, both physical violence and the social violence reflected in the living conditions in which they and their families are forced to survive. While the courses are given by technicians, animators experienced in working with children on the streets supervise the POA and conduct formation sessions. Lucia Gomes, for instance, went on from street work to work as an animator in the POA.

Taking on the authorities

With neighbourhood groups, in which only some children might be workers, the initial focus of discussion is usually the problems of living in their district - the lack of recreational opportunities, lack of money, high levels of criminality or drugs dealing. *"We would encourage the children to think about what was needed in the district and how they could influence what happened there,"* says 'Dino' Raimundo Nonato, an animator at that time. *"For instance one group in a small street in Sacramenta successfully lobbied the municipality to repair the road surface and a derelict access bridge."* Such action helped change the children's self-perception and role in the community; it also influenced local community attitudes towards them.

At one point, children in a nucleus in the Pedreira district were being prevented by meat-stall holders from selling their wares in the market. *"They put their case to the market manager who agreed to work with them, holding monthly meetings with them and calling in their leaders whenever a problem arose. The children proposed some of the rules of this procedure,"* said Sandra, an animator working with the group. *"Some people from the local community also became involved, taking up the children's cause. So the work of the Republic was widely accepted."*

Marisa Pinheiro was one of a team of three animators working with seven groups of children. One was the Limoeiro Street group, some of whose members worked in a busy street market with a major main road running through it. *"It was a very violent place, crowded with traffic and people,"* recalls Marisa. *"People were very aggressive. Drug pushing and muggings were commonplace. There was also a lot of violence between the children - that and the violence in the community was the major focus of discussion."* A number of these children became good leaders in the Republic and, subsequently, part-time volunteers, helping out, for instance, with recreational activities on Saturdays.

Yet another group lived in a street near the headquarters of the Republic. *"They were a street gang (turma). They hung out together. There wasn't then a big problem in Belém of really violent gangs,"* says Marisa Pinheiro. *"Not all of the group worked and they also had problems with drug dealing, glue sniffing and occasional thefts. They were in touch with marginals (people living from crime). Another problem was that because they lived near the Republic's headquarters they came to see it as their space and tended to monopolise the football pitch. We had to talk through all these things with them."*

In Ver-o-Pêso the children took several initiatives to counter violence and harassment at the hands of the police. At the approach of the *Círio de Nazaré*, a major annual festival in Belém, they anticipated intensified police action against them and decided to get assurances from the Governor that they would be left free to work.

By this time the streets around the markets in downtown Belém were becoming crowded with stall holders and petty traders, their numbers swollen by the growing ranks of the unemployed. Relationships between the children on the streets and the market stall holders were deteriorating and accusations that the children were thieves were commonplace. For the first time, pre-adolescent children and girls were beginning to appear among the working children.

The children organised a demonstration outside the Mayor's office and sent a delegation to talk to him. *"They even chose which of the animators they wanted to accompany them. It was Padre Bruno and Lucia Gomes,"* recalls Georgina. But unlike previous demonstrations the adults took no part in the negotiations.

Denise, one of the demonstration leaders, recalls the event: *"We suffered a lot of aggression from the adults in the market and from the* rapa. *The* rapa *would seize our merchandise and give us beatings. The merchandise wasn't ours - we were selling it for other people, so if we lost it, it was a big loss. We made a survey among all the children in Ver-o-Pêso of trouble they had had with the* rapa. *Then we organised a big demonstration to go to the City Hall to deliver our complaints to the Mayor. A boy and I led this demonstration. I was 14 then. I didn't feel afraid. I felt what we were doing was very important and that we would gain dignity by showing people what we were capable of. As usual, the people at the City Hall said the mayor was out of town. We spoke with his representative who promised to deal with our requests. The animators were with us but didn't intervene. After that the* rapa *was a bit less violent towards us. But they tended to pick on me because I had been a leader. There was a regulation that barred us from selling parsley and things inside the market itself but no-one had ever heeded it. The* rapa *began picking on me for that. I told the animators, but they couldn't be with me 24 hours a day. So I had to be more watchful and quicker on my feet. Still, it was a very good initiative even if we didn't win anything permanent from it."*

At this time there were a few other examples of such action by children in Brazil[7]. Though the grassroots nuclei had some victories they also had defeats. There was much distress in the Pedreira group, for instance about a 12-year-old girl who was being routinely sexually abused by a 60-year-old stall holder.

---

[7]Similar action had been taken by children of the Movement of Children and Adolescents (MAC) in Pernambuco in 1980, which the Republic had been aware of in the early days of its development. Founder of the MAC Reginaldo Veloso describes an intervention by the working school-children of the village of Marcacão, who in 1980 successfully lobbied the Mayor of nearby Rio Tinto to withdraw water charges in their village. See *Marcacão 80 or Children in Movement, The long walk of the united children of Marcacão*, Reginaldo Veloso, I.M.A.C./M.I.D.A.D.E., Paris 1982.

"We were not able to solve this case because her family was financially supported by the stall holder and colluded in the abuse. When we tried to approach the man directly he would simply look at us coldly and begin sharpening his knives," recalls Sandra.

Denise's story:
I realised I could make progress without beating others up

"I started working when I was five. I wandered through my neighbourhood trying to sell sweets. When I was eight, we had a financial crisis at home so I went to sell parsley and lemon in Ver-o-Pêso - far from my own district. It was my decision but my mother thought it was great because we needed the money. She told me to go with my brother - he was 10. He took me to Ver-o-Pêso. I looked at the iron market (the meat market constructed with ornate cast iron). I looked at the boats. I knew this was going to be my world from then on. When I started at the market I had nothing in my head. I realised I was nobody. It shocked me that my parents were so absent in my life. I thought my brother could protect me - he wanted to, but he had his own preoccupations. He would leave me alone. I felt totally lonely and I really needed him. A woman who was selling the same things as I started hitting me because I sold more than her. I realised I would have to defend myself - and I started to become very aggressive. I acquired the tools to defend myself - they were my strength, my alertness, my speed and my aggression. In the street you had to be very strong, or you would be caught. If I didn't defend myself, others would profit from me and I wouldn't profit from anything.

"At first I sold bags and vegetables. Then I had to study during the day and would sell gum at night in the bars and the brothels and to the sweethearts in the squares. I met the animators and started going to the Republic just for the lunch. Then I began to realise the importance of the other work, of getting organised in consciousness raising groups, especially when we had a common problem like the rapa.

"The other issue we had to deal with was the harassment of the girls on the streets by the fish sellers in the market and other men. We were 14-15 and they were very attracted to us. So we discussed this in the group. There wasn't much we could do about the harassment. It was everywhere. But it was very important to talk about it with the animators

70

and the group. It led to the idea of our having meetings every two weeks to discuss the body and sexuality. That is how a girls' group came into being. The girls from all the markets of Belém - Ver-o-Pêso, Redondeza, São Brás - all came to the group. Our mothers never talked to us about these things. Our mothers are very remote from our reality. They stay at home and we have a different fate in the streets that they know nothing about. Also they are not educated sexually themselves so they have no knowledge to pass on to us.

"Because the Republic followed us up, we were able to learn to value the woman's body, how to use contraceptives, how to have relationships without getting STDs (sexually transmitted diseases) and other issues.

"We met as a group every Thursday and Saturday. I was elected leader. There were others in the group who could speak up for themselves but I think the boys in the group voted for me because they liked me. I never asked to be a leader but I enjoyed it. I would take the ideas that came up to the meeting of the leaders of the grassroots nuclei.

"The Republic helped me to feel like a person to be valued. I used to be aggressive with everyone. I would have to be the strongest to be sure of getting an advantage. If I wasn't the strongest, I would have to join someone stronger than me. Perhaps if it hadn't been for the animators, I would have gone into prostitution like so many other girls. By helping me to become more conscious, the movement helped me see that I could make progress without being aggressive - without raising my voice, or having to take advantage of everyone, or beating others up. It was through the nuclei that I gained a different awareness of what rights are and what duty is and I began to feel that I was a citizen."

(Denise survived street life and went to work for two years at the state Foundation for Welfare (FBESP), teaching literacy to children. She then won a scholarship to the Federal University to study pedagogy and conduct research into indigenous education in tribal areas.)

Questioning the Salesian link

Early in the '80s there was a deep sense of commitment among the animators who participated in the community experiments at the headquarters, a number

71

of whom were ready to make a lifetime commitment to the movement. They felt that, with its successive generations of children and of young animators, it needed a permanent community at its heart to give it continuity and preserve its spirit. The stumbling block was that formally it was a Salesian undertaking.

As a Salesian, Padre Bruno was bound by special commitments - including obedience to superiors - that were at odds with the core democratic principle of the Republic. Important decisions had to be submitted to the congregation, which was legally responsible for the movement, and had the power to overturn them. Padre Bruno could be posted elsewhere and replaced arbitrarily by another priest. These were problems in principle rather than practice, but the non-Salesians in the core group felt unable to dedicate their lives to something which, in the final count, was subject to the arbitrary control of outsiders. Padre Bruno also passionately believed that when something new was born it should be allowed to develop its own life and identity. The proposal was made and much debated that it was time to cut the link with the congregation. Prolonged negotiations were held with the congregation to try to resolve the problem. An official visitor from the General Council of the Salesians considered whether the movement was compatible with the order's rules and regulations, and found that it was not. The Republic, however, had a following among younger Salesians. At an assembly of the movement, Padre Bruno argued for staying within the Salesian fold. Just as the movement attempted to influence society at large through its actions, so it should strive for greater acceptance among Salesians as an authentic expression of the principles of Don Bosco.

There was another issue. *"From the very beginning Padre Bruno had wanted to demonstrate that Brazilian youth and lay people could undertake this kind of work. He believed we were perfectly able to liberate ourselves,"* says Georgina. *"He has great faith in us and it's still an important issue for him today. He specifically wanted to demonstrate it to the Salesian congregation."*

Padre Bruno's argument for staying with the Salesians prevailed, but the price was the loss of the opportunity to form a permanent community. *"Sometimes I wonder if we might have had an even richer experience had the movement asserted its autonomy at that time,"* he reflects.

Educator Flávia Chagas makes contact with children selling bags at the meat market.

Children and educator Ana Dorotéia Magalhães (left) grab a quick snack outside the restaurant at the Republic.

A member of the girls' group cleans up broken dolls for recycling.

A class in the City of Emmaus School.

Former working child Maria de Nazaré Costa now plans to be a lawyer on behalf of street children.

On the march - a delegate at the Fourth National Meeting of Street Boys and Girls.

Children and adolescents at the Fourth National Meeting head for the Congress.

Padre Bruno Sechi gets a visit from children from the neighbourhood of
the Republic.

Chapter seven

New expressions of the movement

There were other important developments in the Republic in the first half of the '80s, including the initiation of two new work fronts - the City of Emmaus and Children's Legal Defence Centre (CDM), the first such centre in Brazil. Both entailed the mobilisation of new support from the people of Belém.

These developments deepened the Republic's sense of being a movement. The Republic, the Campaign of Emmaus, the CDM and the City of Emmaus were all regarded as autonomous but collaborating 'expressions' of the movement, co-ordinated by a common annual policy making assembly and co-ordinating council.

City of Emmaus

As invasion lands became more densely populated and traffic in and out of the city centre intensified, it became more and more time consuming and impractical to bridge the working and home worlds of many of the children in the movement. The animators of the Republic had been thinking for some time of intensifying their work in the communities from which working children came. A survey conducted by the Republic showed that 70 percent of the children on the city's streets were from one of the most distant suburbs, Bengui, an invasion area some 20km kilometres from the centre.

Ten acres of land under natural bush immediately bordering Bengui was identified by the Republic and donated by supporters in the city. Composed of cheek-by-jowl shanty dwellings, accessed by narrow muddy tracks and bereft of all basic services, the Bengui was then notorious for violence. Its inhabitants were former subsistence farmers and rural workers. Most had been ejected from their land by land barons, or capital developments, or poverty. In fact, Basic Christian Communities[1] were very active in the district, and there was a relatively high degree of community organisation. In 1979 a federation of community organisations in different parts of Belém, including the Bengui, appeared - part of the rising challenge from civil society to dictatorship.

[1] Referred to earlier.

Named the Commission of Poor Districts of Belém (CBB), it mobilised public demonstrations and other actions over land rights and demands for services. By 1981, four years before the dictatorship collapsed, it was able to put 10,000 demonstrators on the streets.

Half of the animators living in the Republic decamped to the new land and began to strengthen their contacts with the local community. Among those to go were Inácia, Padre Bernardo and former street child João Gomes, who was later to become co-ordinator of the CBB and an important leader in the popular movement in Belém. Their first plan, inspired by the Israeli kibbutz experiment, reflected their idealism. It was to establish a new co-operative community of particularly needy families. They decided to call it the City of Emmaus. The families were identified with the help of the Bengui Residents' Association. *Mutirãos (volunteer work parties)* converted farm outbuildings on the land into dwellings, a small health centre and a school room, and prepared some of the land for cultivation and animal raising.

"It was an idea everyone liked," says Inácia. *"Everyone wanted to be involved. Each weekend families would come with their children to help build the houses and the school."* However the naiveté of the plan was soon exposed. Collective production went well enough but, when it came to sharing the produce, there were bitter and divisive quarrels. It was clear to the animators co-ordinating the work that its formulation had been hopelessly over-idealistic. Never frightened to dismantle their mistakes, they called a halt, disbanded the community and entered into more searching discussion with Bengui's community organisers about how to use the land to the community's best advantage.

What the community wanted most was a school. At that time there was just one state elementary school in the district providing for 500 of the many thousands of children. A major CBB demonstration of the time, mobilised around the slogan, 'School For All', reflected the growing importance attached to education by people in poor communities.

For its part, the Republic had become increasingly frustrated by its attempts to assure the children it worked with of an education. Mainstream education, deriving from inappropriate European models translated to Brazil under colonialism, had never been attuned to the circumstances and priorities of children living in poverty. Inflexible, authoritarian and, under the dictatorship, technically oriented, the system failed to recognise that many children were forced to work to support themselves and their families. Teachers, who were desperately under-paid, under-resourced and in many cases poorly trained, had neither the skills nor the patience to respond to their educational problems, their difficulties in sticking strictly to school schedules or their parents' inability to pay for their books and uniforms.

"Schools really did everything they could to exclude these children," says Graça. *"The biggest problem of all was the teachers' attitudes. Teachers and principals regarded such children as inferior and incapable of being educated. A child who works on the streets acquires a taste for freedom and learns to fend for himself. He won't tolerate aggression or do everything he is told. If he is shouted at he will swear back. The children reproduce the violence they are exposed to and the only response of the school system was to pile on yet more violence in the form of punishment and rejection. The Republic had done all kinds of things to get children into school - we even supplied uniforms and books and obtained documents for them - but our efforts were being thwarted mainly by the school system itself. The children simply couldn't bear being in school. They tended to get typecast as rebels and then get expelled or leave of their own volition."*

Just as the Republic had set out to expose the failure of the state by creating a new liberating response to children on the streets, the City of Emmaus now wanted to create a school that would both demonstrate the ability of poor children and the abject failure of the state school system in excluding them.

The animators from the City of Emmaus set out to involve the children, their parents and community in helping define the educational priorities of the new school and to engage their active participation in its development. The very idea of a school designed for its users with their participation was totally revolutionary. It was a pioneering attempt to decentralise and democratise educational provision at the grassroots and chimed with the mounting broader challenge by union and community leaders to dictatorship in Brazil.

Securing the participation of parents and of a community quite unaccustomed to being consulted was easier to talk about than achieve. Schooled in oppression and denied educational opportunities themselves, many in the community assumed that such specialised matters were best left to the 'experts'.

"To elicit their views we would discuss with them all the things they didn't like about the schools they knew, including the attitudes towards them of principals

and teachers," says Georgina. *"On the basis of those experiences we would propose a different kind of school, one they did seem to like."* The animators proposed a school that would pay its respects to the traditional knowledge and rural origins of the local people - knowledge devalued by the consumerist and other priorities of the city. They spoke of an education which would develop the children's' capacity to act as citizens and understand and support the community's struggle for its rights. These ideas were warmly welcomed. By such means, some level of participation was achieved.

In planning the school and in developing its educational model, the movement again demonstrated its readiness to seek outside advice and its ability to pull in the enthusiastic support of professional people in the city with a range of relevant skills. A support group was formed. It included a civil engineer and an educationist, Ana Maria Tancredi, of the Federal University in Belém, who was both an activist in the popular movement and an expert in Montessori methods.

Educating for a better society

Everything about the school that emerged from this process was strikingly different. Even its physical structure was something new. People would come out from the city just to look at it. Government schools in poor areas were small utilitarian brick boxes under asbestos roofing, which heated up like ovens in the tropical climate. By contrast, the classrooms at the City of Emmaus are independent circular structures, distributed in spacious park-like surroundings, and covered with cool thatch, open under the eves to allow a free flow of air. They are of Amazonian Indian design, affirming the culture of the people who make up the majority of the local population. At the same time, the fact that they are circular is perfectly suited to an educational approach that emphasises pupil participation. There is no front or back to a round classroom - no lead position and no corners to be sent to stand in. No-one sits behind anyone else. The space can be used in a variety of ways. *"The children can use whatever they want in the space, they can even lie down on the floor and copy something there if they want to,"* says teacher Maria Jose Castro.

As in the movement's street-based work, the quality of the relationship between the teachers and children is seen to be fundamental to the educational process. The teacher here is friend, guide and facilitator. *"He or she has more systematic knowledge than the child,"* says Graça, *"but the child also has information and experience and this is recognised and valued in the educational process. The transaction between children and teachers is that of sharing."* The teachers gain in many different ways, personally in their reorientation to the rejected underclass, professionally in learning how to work with deprived children.

The child-centred approach of the school draws on the Republic's own experience with working children as well as from Paulo Freire, Don Bosco and Montessori. *"We used to joke that we had married Don Bosco to Maria Montessori,"* says Georgina, who came over to the school from the Republic during the '80s to take responsibility for its educational orientation. *"Don Bosco, because of the relationship we offer to the child. Maria Montessori, for the richness of the educational materials. Paulo Freire and our own street experience gave us the concept of education that starts from the child's own reality and develops with the child's active participation."*

Few commercial or official educational materials are used. *"Books sent to us from São Paulo depicted a model middle-class, nuclear family with European-looking children enjoying the resources and activities of the middle class. They contained nothing children in Bengui could relate to. They were a denial of their reality,"* says Graça. *"We might have a child whose only family was a grandmother, and yet this family could well have the same emotional value that we attribute to the nuclear family. In the City of Emmaus school, educational materials - text, illustrations, models - are made up with the children's participation, reflecting the pedagogical principle of building the child's knowledge and capacity to learn outwards from his or her own experience. The first materials made are composed from children's accounts of their own lives, families and local community, and are designed to reinforce the child's sense of identity and membership of a class and community. From describing their own families, the children will go on to talk about families in general, why families are important and the difficulties they face."*

These accounts are deepened and strengthened in the curriculum by explorations of the children's world through social studies classes. In the latter, the children explore their own neighbourhood and visit other neighbourhoods, comparing what they find. From there they will go on to learn about other cities and countries. There is an emphasis on learning by doing, reinforcing the children's sense of building their own knowledge - including by means of games and role play. *"It is an active form of education well suited to the child who, coming in from the violence and stress of the streets, would find it intolerable to sit still for any period of time, regimented in straight rows,"* says Graça.

From their work on the streets, the animators had gained a good understanding of the emotional needs and the lives and commitments of working children. The school was not rigid about their keeping to a schedule, respecting the fact that they had other responsibilities. It maintained a direct and informal relationship with parents. A teacher who became concerned about a child's failure to attend class would go to talk with the parents and find out what the problem was and how it might best be overcome. School uniforms were dispensed with because many parents simply couldn't afford them. As it was, children did not always have all the items of clothing they needed.

"Sometimes a child will come here to say they can't attend because they have no shoes or they haven't a shirt. We will tell them, 'It's not your shoes or your shirt that is going to learn. It's you! So come on in,' " says Maria Jose Castro.

The school's admissions policy reversed general practice by giving priority to the very children usually excluded from school - those from families with the fewest resources. Many who attended would be regarded by the educational system as ineducable and as problem children, but punishment played no part in the pedagogy of affirmation and participation practised by the school. There was no ominous collecting of the names, or derision of children who committed a disturbance during a class. No-one was routinely singled out and ordered out of the class room. Problems were talked through with the children and where appropriate with their families. The culture of the school emphasised freedom and responsibility rather than restriction. The children took part in regular evaluations of the education they were receiving and their own contribution to it. They were allowed free access to the grounds, freedom to pick the fruit of the forest and no part of the school was closed to them. That said, a few children were so damaged by their experience that they needed a more intensively therapeutic environment than the school was able to offer. Until recently there was a programme in Belém to which such children could be referred.

The Production Centre

Though the idea of building a community of poor people on the land at Bengui was abandoned, the name 'City of Emmaus' was retained as representing the city of the dreams of those involved.

Apart from the establishment of the school, agricultural activity continued to be practised, initially to provide food for the restaurant at the Republic and meals at the school. The work was at first done on a voluntary basis by the animators, who continued to live at the City of Emmaus, as well as by people from the neighbourhood. Food surplus to the movement's needs, was sold. A proportion of the resulting income was distributed among the neighbourhood helpers. Later, as inflationary costs ate into available income, production efficiency was stepped up with the help of university advisors. The Production Unit, as this area of activity was called, became a key income earner for the City of Emmaus. Employees were taken on, drawn from the local community. Jaime who was away from the Republic for some years, working in Amazonia, returned to manage the unit.

In addition to the cultivation of vegetables and raising of poultry and pork, a medicinal herb garden and small dispensary were created[2], providing cheap, effective medication that affirmed the traditional knowledge of the mainly Indian people in the area.

The Production Unit also developed an educational section known as the Production School, essentially an accessory of the main school. Teachers took their pupils to the Production School to relate maths and science to real life situations familiar to children with a recent rural past. Maths, for instance, might be applied to the practical problems of assessing feed quantities for the animals or the dimensions of an area to be cultivated, or the planning of a new chicken house. A small number of children, however, were also students of the Production School, attending it when the main school classes were over. Among them were children otherwise most likely to end up on the streets as well as the least self-disciplined children, who found it easier to develop a sense of responsibility and progress through practical activities. The children were given what they produced in the Production School, either for sale or family consumption and this small income helped their families release them from income earning obligations.

---

[2] This was achieved with advice from The North-east Centre for Popular Medicine of Dr Celerino Carriconde and Diana Mores, who are internationally known for their promotion of traditional medicine and who assist popular organisations throughout the north and north-east to establish herbal medicine gardens. The service illustrates the diversity of the popular movement in Brazil.

The Production School did not offer occupational training, though it developed skills, such as poultry rearing, that could procure supplementary income. The only occupational tuition offered in the City of Emmaus was cabinet making and carpentry, a skill much in demand in Bengui, where most informal dwellings were constructed of wood.

Striking an agreement with government

As the School of Emmaus set out to recruit children from the neediest families, a fee-paying basis for attendance was out of the question. The alternative, to be some kind of public school, would involve the movement in its first contractual agreement with the state. There was a danger of being co-opted, but the movement now felt well enough established to be able to protect itself.

In the event, it managed to strike an unprecedented agreement with the Department of Education, SEDUC. The department agreed to provide teachers and pay their salaries, as well as those of the instructors in the Production School, while the City of Emmaus retained total control over the methodology used and was responsible for the maintenance of the grounds and buildings. It was a pioneering example of organised civil society claiming a role in determining public policy.

In practice, the relationship proved to be one in which the school had continually to angle, within the straitjacket of departmental priorities and regulations, for the space to prove its educational thesis. There was a mismatch, for instance, between teachers' working conditions, as established by the state, and the special needs of the school. The school's emphasis on the relationship between teacher and child, the additional work involved in making original educational materials, maintaining a relationship with parents and involvement in the community, all demanded the spirit of the volunteer rather than the employee. To make space for such additional activities, the school had to sacrifice some subjects it would like to have included in the syllabus. The student-teacher ratios proscribed by the department (currently 40-1) were double those suited to the school's educational approach. The authoritarian attitudes and practice of teachers trained and supplied by the state were and remain inappropriate to the liberating practice of the school. *"In conventional schools,"* says Graça, by way of illustration, *"there is a big emphasis on control of the children. They are virtually under arrest. In our school the emphasis is on freedom. On joining us, some teachers are either too authoritarian or they go overboard in the other direction, confusing freedom and licence."* There have been teachers who let children go swimming in the river rather than attend class.

Even basic aspects of methodology presented problems. Classrooms at the school were subject specific, developed as resource centres which the child helped to create and explored. In the history class there would be objects of historical interest, including the local community history, maps, models, illustrations, materials developed or collected by the teachers and the children, as well as books. *"The child participates in the making of the environment,"* says Ana Tancredi, who developed the application of the Montessori methods in the school and became its principal. *"The idea is to give the child a choice of what to do and the teacher's role is to stimulate the child to organise his or her own learning. So the teacher needs to be flexible and varied in her approach. Chalk and blackboard are demoted as instruments of education."*

Ana Tancredi worked for the school on a voluntary basis and trained the first batch of teachers. They were selected from the local community, something she now regards as being over-idealistic. *"We brought a very good Montessori teacher from São Paulo and had 150 hours of training but the teachers were still a bit uncertain,"* she recalls. *"For instance, I was discussing with them the ideas of an Argentinean educator about the democratic teacher and the policeman teacher. They all wanted to be the democratic teacher but weren't too sure how. You don't learn that from one day to another, so there were some difficulties in the beginning. Also I think the moment my back was turned they would go back to their old ways and leap for the safety of the blackboard. If I was going to do it again I would make a more thorough investment in teacher training."*

Most state-trained teachers also needed political preparation. *"Many were very unaware of the world they lived in,"* says Graça. *"They had been trained during the dictatorship and had no concept of education for a better society. They didn't consider families in a political, economic and social context. If a child had problems it was the child's own fault or that of the family. Also they had never considered the political implications of how they taught, or even that it had any political implications. We had to work to get them to review their role in society and to understand that unless they changed their way of working they would be contributing to the very processes that excluded the poorer layers of society from their basic rights and from realising their status as citizens. Here, we made it clear, the thrust of the work was different - it was exactly to awaken in the children the sense of their own citizenship, of both their rights and responsibilities."*

To try to bridge the gap between the state's teacher training and the school's requirements, the school had to create its own training programme. Training was not limited to a course. It was something also realised on a day-to-day basis in the way the school operated and in interchanges between staff, children and parents.

Graça offers an illustration of the point. She had been away from the Republic for nearly 10 years, taking a degree and then making a family. She returned to become director of the new school and found that she had lots of relearning to do herself, including working through an authoritarian tendency in herself which had been reinforced during her time at university.

One day she spotted a teacher wearing dark glasses in class. *"I had a word with her. I told her it was quite wrong to be wearing sunglasses. She had to have eye-to-eye contact with the children. The school then worked with themes and at that time was working with the theme of violence. The teacher started crying and removed her glasses to reveal terribly bruised eyes. She told me that morning she had been raped and beaten up by her husband. I felt deeply ashamed. She had been talking with the children about the violence in society at the very moment in which she was a victim of it. So we caught the moment to talk the following day with the children about this violence which is directed against children and women, those least able to defend themselves. She set her glasses aside and spoke without fear or shame. We discussed why there is such violence and how we might work to rid society of it. After the talk, several girls came to the teacher to tell about abuse that they had undergone. It was a very rich moment from which we all learned. Our training has never been limited to the subject or to a particular schedule. We are ready to put everything into the classroom and we learn through lived experience."*

The school's control over the selection of its teachers has fluctuated with departmental policy, but has always been subject to the constraint that not many teachers are keen to work in Bengui anyway. At times it has had no choice but to accept teachers allocated to it by the department. Some become converts to its special educational approach, some cannot adapt and leave, while others continue to teach there but without the necessary commitment. As a result, the degree to which the school can realise its goals fluctuates, and can take a real dip if several valued teachers decide to leave at more or less the same time.

The school set out to provide children with four years of education, after which they would go on to ordinary state schools. The difficulties they faced, however, in adapting to a very different educational environment and values persuaded the school to add a further four years. *"Our children were not submissive enough and asked too many questions,"* said Georgina. *"We encourage them to express themselves and talk freely with the teachers or the principal. State schools have tended to regard them as strange or undisciplined. Most now stay on here till standard eight."*

In 1984 it was decided, in dialogue with the residents' associations, to ensure a supply of appropriately trained teachers by developing a small high school specifically to train elementary school teachers.

At this time an activist group of teachers from various other schools had, on their own initiative, launched an access course, enabling students from poor communities to win places at the Federal University. The City of Emmaus was able to secure the help of this group in elaborating its new teacher training course and in training its first teachers.

Among the group was Ana Sgrott. She became teacher in the high school and developed a new methodology for the teaching of science and maths - using resources of the Production School and the Bengui community. *"Basically we developed in science and maths the methodology used in the elementary school, which builds on the child's own knowledge,"* says Ana. Working with the trainee teachers, she also developed an experimental science and maths laboratory. The school's science projects have repeatedly won recognition in annual municipal Science Fairs which are promoted state-wide.

Establishing links with the community

Though the City of Emmaus directly borders Bengui, it is not in the heart of it. Various strategies have been tried to engage with the community. The animators participate in the local residents' associations and popular organisations and take part in the community's struggles and in traditional celebrations. Conversely people from the community are invited to the city to participate in events and discussions at the City of Emmaus. The school holds evening adult education classes. There are community representatives on the school board and parents are encouraged to take an active interest in the school. On Sunday, *Domingo Alegri* (Happy Sunday) - a celebratory event equivalent to the Oratory - provides catechism classes, sports, cultural and other recreational activities, which are open equally to pupils at the school and other children from the community.

From the children's point of view, the neighbourhood is an extension of their classroom and issues of community interest are material for their education. Within a programme, *Science for the Community*, the children investigated the contamination of underground water in Bengui. *"We made a statistical survey of the sanitation conditions in the district - human waste disposal, water quality, water use and disposal, the types of wells used,"* recalls Ana Sgrott. *"We filmed the children interviewing local people and we discussed with them what was done with garbage and human waste and why water treatment is important. We developed a model. We undertook other activities related to water, soil, air and so on - drawing on the sciences, mathematics and social studies, as well as communication and expression - but always bridging the educational content with the conditions of the children's lives.*

"The findings were then reported to the local residents' association as a basis for its struggle for better services. We also tried to link up with the Federal University, inviting it to investigate the possibility of introducing a water system used to good effect elsewhere."

In another project that produced valuable feedback for the community, the children investigated how the remnants of corpses, disinterred prematurely from the cemetery to make way for new arrivals, were being dumped in the open along with supermarket and other waste. A video made by the school showed child waste collectors using human bones to probe the dump. The film was shown to the residents' association, debated with the community and used to support community pressure on the city authorities to deal with the problem.

The school's influence

The school began to attract visitors from other parts of Brazil and from other countries. University students came and still come on extension assignments to study its educational philosophy and methodology. Because of the attention given the children, the problem endemic in Brazil of children having to repeat grades has not been a feature of the school of the City of Emmaus. Elements of the school's approach have been applied elsewhere - even the style of its classrooms has been copied, if mainly because they are cheap to construct. The school has also had an impact through its students and teachers who have gone on to other schools and activities; ex-pupils include a congressman and activists in workers' and community organisations.

Hitting back at violence: Brazil's first Children's Legal Defence Centre

The Children's Legal Defence Centre (CDM) started by the movement in Belém opened up an important new front against the social abandonment of children. While the Republic and City of Emmaus prepared children to have a transforming influence in society, the aim of the CDM was to mobilise legal and academic clout to promote and reinforce their rights.

The CDM was instituted in 1983 as the animators realised they were not equipped to deal with the violence that continually threatened the well-being and the lives of the children with whom they were trying to work. The life of the CDM began - as with the other initiatives of the movement - with the mobilising of potential supporters in the city who possessed the necessary skills. Maria Luiza (Lu) Lamaro, a former volunteer, played a key role in establishing the CDM and became its first co-ordinator. In setting it up, she consulted with the Brazilian Bar Association (OAB) in Belém, drew up a dossier of cases of violence against children and invited lawyers to attend a seminar on October 10, Human Rights Day. The invitation bore the message, 'We need lawyers'. In fact the seminar was also attended by doctors, social workers and psychologists interested in doing something. Two children from the Republic spoke at the seminar, one describing how he had been tortured by the police. A few lawyers offered their services as advisors.

The aims of the CDM were to intervene in specific cases of violence, publicly expose violence, denounce the failure of the authorities to act against violence and to mobilise public support for the scrapping of the Minor's Code[3]. As mentioned earlier, the Code reflected a strong public security preoccupation and was seen to stigmatise the children of the poor, underpinning the impunity with which they were treated by the police and members of the public.

Seventy percent of the children arrested by the former Children's Police Department in terms of the Code were rounded up on grounds of 'suspicious

---

[3] See next chapter.

behaviour'. The fact that children were entitled to no legal representation and that children's judges could detain them for an indeterminate period defined them as people without rights and as virtually disposable. Children on the streets were exposed to arbitrary arrest and temporary detention in adult jails, to beatings and even torture at the hands of the police, who acted without fear of being called to account. The killing of adolescents in the course of police investigations was nothing out of the ordinary.

Terre des Hommes money was used to hire a secretary, lawyer, psychologist and social worker for the CDM. The rates of pay were so low that the professionals were virtually acting as volunteers, working for the CDM half the day and in the other half employed at the university. In the absence of any provision for the legal representation of children and adolescents, the only way a lawyer might act for a child was if the parents signed over power of attorney. *"Our lawyer used to walk around with power of attorney documents in his pocket,"* says Lu.

Given the poor chances of legal action against the police succeeding, the CDM worked also by denouncing violence through the media and other means. Its first murder case was the killing by a fireman of a boy suspected of burglary. The boy, Lindomar Royal do Nascimento, had been running away when he was shot in the leg. He fell and was then shot in the head. A companion was arrested. The CDM pressed for the case to be investigated. Finally it was the subject of a much publicised mock tribunal in Teresina, organised by a committee of the National Movement of Street Boys and Girls[4] of Piaui, with lawyers role-playing the parts. The tribunal was an advocacy technique used elsewhere by the popular movement in land struggles. Attended by people from all over Brazil, the tribunal found the state and civil society guilty of the killing. Though Padre Bruno was subjected to death threats, the CDM pressed home the case until action was taken against the boy's killer. Early opponents of violence against children met with scant public respect; they were even accused of protecting criminals[5].

---

[4] See below.

[5] Another case to be given the mock tribunal treatment included the notorious attack in São Paulo on Joilson. The boy was kicked to death in the streets by a court official after he allegedly tried to steal a neck-chain. Bishop Dom Luciano Mendes of the Minors' Pastorate in São Paulo had difficulty finding a venue for the boy's funeral ceremony which was finally held in the pastorate's own children's home. There was extensive press coverage and Dom Luciano suffered severe criticism for conducting the burial service.

From the beginning, the CDM saw its role as dealing both with cases referred to it through the movement and others which it identified from press reports. It operated from a house donated to the movement. Its governing council was composed of the elected co-ordinators of the other expressions of the movement. In addition, animators of the City of Emmaus and the Republic were specially appointed to liaise with it.

With his increasing contact with other groups and cities throughout Brazil, Padre Bruno, among others, did much to promote the idea of defence centres for children's rights, as did Lu. In 1985, A Centre for the Legal Defence of Children and Adolescents was established in Macapá, Amapá. This centre was to collaborate with the CDM in Belém in promoting defence centres.

Defence Centres appeared in a growing number of cities in the latter half of the '80s, eventually forming a National Network. They were active in the mobilisation for new legislation for children's rights and have played a key role in the development and implementation of children's rights. They collaborate with and, where necessary, exert pressure on government to act in accordance with the law in prosecuting contraventions of children's rights. They undertake action-oriented research as a basis for their campaigning. They are advocates for the interests of children. In particular they have set out to combat the impunity with which violence is directed at children and adolescents. They also try to raise the profile of children's rights within the legal and associated professions and among students of law and the social sciences.

Despite their importance, the CDM and subsequent defence centres are not involved directly in the participation and organisation of children and so this book will not consider them in more depth.

Chapter eight

Forming a National Movement of Street Boys and Girls

Coming out of isolation

Before 1979, when the International Year of the Child spotlighted the plight of working children, most governments failed to acknowledge their existence[1]. Even after that they began to do so only reluctantly. The Brazilian government was no exception and in that same year introduced the Minors' Code. Community organisations were sharply critical of the new law which was likely to preserve oppressive and paternalistic public responses to deprived children and left decisions about them in the hands of the judges. UNICEF Brazil, an agency that had the trust of the authorities, also offered no support for the Code. The following year a more progressive director was appointed President of FUNABEM, the centralised government agency responsible for children and adolescents in difficult circumstances. She made a short-lived attempt to reform the organisation from the top but provoked too much internal hostility and was sacked for her troubles.

By 1981, there was some loosening up in government, reflecting preparations by the military in a carefully controlled way to return the country to civilian government[2]. Within the Secretariat for Social Action, in the Ministry of Welfare, officials were beginning to recognise that government policy of institutionalising children was not working. But they had no idea about what else to do. They decided to seek UNICEF's advice. A senior UNICEF official, Bill Myers, was seconded to the Ministry as advisor to the Secretary for Social Action. *"There were now new people coming into government - technocrats or idealists wanting to do something,"* says Myers. *"The government was losing its anti-Communist cohesion - there were people who realised that such obsessions made for over-oppressive government. So it was still authoritarian but no longer really oppressive."*

---

[1] *A Global Overview of Social Mobilisation on Behalf of Street Children*, Peter Tacon.

[2] A year later, for the first time since the military seized power in 1964, voters were able to elect national, state and municipal representatives.

Before coming to Brazil, Myers had seen US press coverage of what were then assumed to be large numbers of abandoned children on the streets of the country's major cities. UNICEF as yet had no programme for children in difficult circumstances but had recently appointed a special consultant on the subject at its headquarters in New York, Peter Tacon, the founder of Child Hope. In Brazil the issue was still very sensitive. On taking up his new post, Myers found no mention of such children in government planning and policy documents, which focused instead on children in institutions. He raised the matter. Despite a continuing denial of the problem by the state, the Secretary for Social Action was interested in looking into it.

In March 1981, in an unprecedented move, a senior UNICEF/Government team set out to investigate the situation at first hand. They visited states where the problem of abandoned children was thought likely to be most severe. It was the first step in a process that would help transform both government and UNICEF policies towards marginalised children.

The team members were Miltes Santa Cruz of the Secretariat for Social Action, Sonia Maria da Silva, then assistant to the President of FUNABEM, Bill Myers and Peter Tacon from UNICEF in New York. Their exploration curiously echoes further up the social pyramid that of the volunteers who went to the streets of Belém more than 10 years earlier and discovered working children. They also discovered children. For Miltes Santa Cruz the trip was a revelation. *"We felt like explorers of a whole new territory,"* she says. Peter Tacon kept striking up conversations with children on the streets, drawing attention to them and asking what the government was doing about them. *"We felt profoundly embarrassed,"* she says. *"It was as though these children had been invisible to us until then."* In addition, through church networks, they discovered a number of non-government programmes working pretty much in isolation from each other with children on the streets of various cities. Some 70 such programmes were identified, of which nine were of particular interest.

The team held a meeting with the nine. Among them were the Republic of Small Vendors, represented by Padre Bruno, and two other Salesian programmes - Pro-Menor Don Bosco in Manaus and the Salesian Centre for the Minor (CESAM), which operated an occupational training programme in Belo Horizonte, and the Minors' Pastorate which was developing street level programmes in São Paulo.

90

The team announced that it wished to develop a new approach to working with children on the streets and needed their advice. The idea of senior state policy planners openly seeking the advice of community-based organisations was extraordinary and the latter were profoundly mistrustful. They were also very angry about the government handling of socially abandoned children. *"There had been years and years of manipulation on the part of the government, so their suspicion was understandable,"* says Santa Cruz. *"Some thought that we wanted to take advantage of their work. In fact we ourselves at times wondered if we were co-opting them. But we concluded we were not. We saw ourselves as committed to working for a more equitable society."*

Because it had always related to government, UNICEF, referred to satirically by some people as the United States Committee for Children, was equally mistrusted. The team members, however, convinced the nine of their personal sincerity and openness to new ideas. The initiative proceeded on the basis of trusting the individuals in the team rather than the institutions for which they worked. The representatives of the nine non-government organisations were also very curious to get to know more about each other. *"It was very sincere,"* says Padre Bruno of the first meeting. *"We were able to say openly that our aim was to discredit state policy for children and we agreed to participate in a programme that would allow the different experiences in Brazil to meet and communicate with each other."*

Because of its past refusal to have dealings with the state, the Republic's involvement was an important marker for other community-based and non-government organisations who suspected that the initiative was just another government ploy to subvert organisations seeking social change. Government credibility was reinforced by the appointment by UNICEF Brazil of Cesare de Florio la Rocca, a former priest who had worked with street children in Manaus both as a non-government activist and, subsequently, for the State of Amazonia. La Rocca became co-ordinator of the government team.

The last thing the team members wanted to do was create another project for street children, which at that time would simply have been replicated throughout the country. They were clear about one thing: centralised planning had failed. The team was opposed to government assuming sole responsibility for street and working children.

It should rather set out to strengthen local voluntary organisations[3] which would do a better and a much cheaper job. A flaw in this thinking was that the more progressive NGOs had no intention of simply allowing government to fob its responsibilities off on to them. Their aim was to expose the destructiveness of government policy, by both denouncement and exemplifying better practice, and in so doing strengthen growing public demand for accountable government. To do that more effectively, they were now keen to strengthen their own organisation.

Meanwhile, the more progressive newcomers within government were facing the problem of the state's own massive centralised child welfare bureaucracies. These 'Bastilles', these 'monuments to the dictatorship's culture of waste', as advocates of change variously called them, operated within a Brazilian tradition of political patronage and institutional self-interest. Clearly there was no way of changing them by administrative decree, even had the team known what changes to recommend. Instead of attempting a frontal attack, the change makers hit on a strategy of stimulating within them a culture of new thought and practice which would do battle with and eventually overcome the old - in Myers's phrasing, 'a policy dissonance'[4]. For this new thought and practice they looked to the non-government organisations.

"The Secretary knew he would be up against the whole machinery of bureaucratic and political vested interests and old ideas which permeated government welfare bureaucracies and the schools of social work," says Myers. What he wanted from UNICEF was its name to validate investment in popular alternative responses to what was still a very sensitive situation.

Alternative Services for Street Children Project

The device by which the team set about realising its various goals was the joint UNICEF/government Alternative Services for Street Children Project[5]. The team asked the nine non-government organisations it had identified what difficulties they faced and what they needed to strengthen and replicate their work. Their answers determined the support offered by the Project.

---

[3] *Exploring New Paths: Innovative approaches to combating child labour,* Jo Boyden and William Myers ILO, Geneva and ICDC, Florence.

[4] *Alternative Services for Street Children Project: The Brazilian Approach,* William Myers, in *Combating Child Labour.* Ed Assefa Bequele and Jo Boyden ILO, Geneva 1988

[5] Hereafter referred as the Project or Alternative Services Project.

92

The Project provided support for training, research, a communications network, meetings and exchange visits between people active in the field in different cities. It staged five-day training workshops around the country, which included visits by street educators or animators to local programmes. In each workshop there were always a few participants from other parts of the country and there was a mix of people from non-government and community organisations and government employees working with children who wished to attend. The team played a facilitating rather than a providing role. No funding was made available to organisations through the project and training was done mainly by the non-government pioneers of new approaches.

The backbone of the Alternative Services Project was that it provided strong networking, information and communications support. It answered inquiries, put people in touch with each other, produced a bulletin, made videos and films and operated an audio-visual data bank. It also produced a cheap range of 'how to' publications on aspects of work with children, based on what emerged in the workshops, including the distillation of a dialogue between Paulo Freire and street educators[6].

Achievements of the Alternative Services Project

The Project allowed an intensive exchange of ideas that were essentially subversive of the status quo and in sympathy with the gathering tidal wave of public demand for democracy that was to culminate in the military's withdrawal from government.

Like some other organisations, the Republic in Belém was deluged with visitors. *"It was like a beehive. In fact, we had too many visitors for the good of our work,"* recalls Padre Bruno. *"We made a point of revealing to visitors both the strengths and limitations of our work and asking for their impressions so that we, too, could learn from them. Through these visits, which lasted several days, we began to get a more global view of the problems of children on the streets and of the causes. It was very rewarding to find other people with the same concerns as ourselves. We also learned from other programmes*

---

[6] The term 'street educator' was employed by the Minors' Pastorate in São Paulo to describe their outreach workers with children on the streets. The Republic resisted it on the basis that 'educator' implied a one-way transfer of knowledge. It preferred 'volunteer', with its emphasis on voluntary action, and subsequently 'animator' as a more accurate reflection of the activity. 'Street educator' became the dominant term, however, and the Republic capitulated.

- for instance the Meeting Room (in Belo Horizonte) was strong on occupational training and we applied some of their ideas in our workshops, although we did not agree with their political orientation." Of the other programmes it encountered, the Republic identified most with the work of the Minors' Pastorate in São Paulo, and later in other centres. The Pastorate was also trying to extract principles for its work from its engagement with children on the streets rather than starting out from a preconceived idea of what assistance to provide.

Many of the ideas that emerged from the participants in the Alternative Project were eventually to inform changes in the law and public policy. Among them were that:

- Protecting and meeting the needs of all children are a top priority of society;
- The primary purpose of social policy and programmes for children should be their well-being (as opposed to the security of the public);
- Children should participate as subjects of their own development and not as objects of welfare and other interventions by adults, and so should be enabled to be actively engaged in decisions affecting them;
- Services should be developed locally where they could be attuned to local needs and circumstances;
- Government should be restructured so that instead of formulating policy for children centrally it could enable local communities to become involved in addressing the needs of children at risk.

Many new assistance projects for street, working and poor community children came into being, some working with the ideas of children as subjects of their own development and initiating their work within the children's social reality - that of the squares, streets and peripheral districts in which they lived[7]. The role of the animators, or street educators as they came to be known, gained wide recognition, the training of such educators becoming a priority of the Project.

The Project's workshops led to the formation around the country of some 35 activist groups of people working with children in both non-government and government agencies. These groups were to play a key role in the formation of

---

[7] *Brazil's National Street Children's Movement, a brief history* by Benedito Rodrigues dos Santos.

a National Movement of Street Children and in a widespread mobilisation of public support in favour of children's rights.

In time, the ideas released through the project also produced some substantial changes in government practice, with more progressive programmes emerging in the latter half of the '80s in São Paulo, Recife and Goiânia. The ability of the state institutions, however, really to embrace the principles of the participation and organisation of children is still doubted by NGOs. For that to happen would imply government in the service of the people, including the most powerless.

"We never really understood the motivation of the heads of the institutions which sponsored the Alternative Project," says Padre Bruno. *"Antonio Carlos Gomes da Costa[8] has said that from an Alternative Services proposal it did become an altering one. I don't know to what extent the process that flowed from the Project has really altered the views of the heads of those institutions or of state governors. Are they any closer to understanding that street children are the product of an unjust social structure and that fundamental changes have to be made?*

"My view is that aspects of our work were appropriated mechanically by the state institutions and even some of the NGOs, without the fundamentally libertarian philosophy that breathes spirit into them and proposes social change. For instance they copied the ideas of co-operatives for working children but not as a form of political organisation and consciousness raising. It is very difficult to translate such a philosophy into the institutional sphere. Maybe a number of good educators and technicians in the state enterprises did find ways to insinuate it into their work."

One NGO view of the Project was that it was originally a lifeline thrown by morally bankrupt state institutions to rescue themselves from their isolation from the community as the country moved towards democracy. It enabled them to transform their rhetoric from that of control into that of participation and empowerment of civil society. The members of the Project team were at first marginal within their institutions, but as they gained command over a more modern language, they became the leading edge, steadily winning ground, until the new-speak became the official language. But the new language also opened

---

[8]A progressive manager of public policy and educationalist who has been highly influential in the struggle for children rights in Brazil.

conceptual space for the development of better practice. A new culture was indeed introduced into them. *"Within government institutions today, there is a gradation of people, from those who struggle hard to support a fundamentally new approach to those who clothe old ways in the new speech,"* says Benedito Rodrigues dos Santos, an intellectual activist who became prominent in the movement for children's rights and who had been working with deprived youth in the city of Goiânia since 1978.

In the final account, both the representatives of non-government organisations most committed to tackling the causes and the symptoms of children's suffering and government workers who shared their ideas found the Alternative Project constraining and the degree of participation it offered circumscribed.

Dos Santos contextualises its place in the development of thought about children's rights. *"Before 1930, we had a predominance of religious explanations for the child on the streets. This child was regarded as paying for the sins of his family. From 1930 we began to get more scientific explanations, but still very functionalistic, rooted in American anthropology and the psychology of those days. Delinquency was explained as a product of personality or character, but these new interpretations had the virtue of contradicting the magical explanation of the church. Then we began to get the explanation of oppressed children as being the fruit of unstructured or dismantled families, but with no explanation of why these families were distressed. The view of the child as the accused began to change to one of the child as victim but still the victim of isolated structures, the family or something else - migration or unemployment - taken out of context. But, from the '70s onwards and after the dictatorship, we were able to establish the whole framework of the socio-political context.*

*"In the Alternative Project, the emphasis was on pedagogy without a clear political dimension. For instance, they would describe street children but would not analyse the context that generated the poverty in these children. They would talk about children's work and how to stimulate income-generating projects and would teach children ways of making soap or ice-cream. They seemed to want children to work to support their families. We felt the investment should be in getting children into school. We wanted to discuss why these children had to work at all. We wanted to know why, if children were having to help their families survive, were the families not demanding better survival conditions? Our question was - **were these children not being forced to help maintain the unjust economic system we were living***

96

in? Such differences of perspective created a tension in the Alternative Services Project."

"I never discount the importance of this project," says Padre Bruno. *"The information exchange helped in the pedagogical development of many organisations. Many aspects of methodology and direct assistance to children were discussed and systematised. For instance, we studied in depth the relationship between educator and child and such things as the approach on the streets. These are important issues even today. But today it is much clearer to us that all these issues ought to be worked out within the greater objective of strengthening the organisation of the children and locating their organisation within the greater organisation of oppressed people in general. Within the Project there was little debate about the organisation of children, because when you talk about organisation you go directly to talk about politics. There was a tendency to overemphasise one aspect, as there is in the way UNICEF works generally. For example, they emphasised income-generating projects for children, building on a distortion of what should be real opportunities for children in society. A solution will never be achieved in that way.*

"The political dimension of the work with children was not developed through the Alternative Services Project. It may partly be due to the fact that it was still quite early on in the opening up period."

Another concern of some participants in Alternative Services Project was that it mobilised only practitioners. They were being drawn into formulating policy ideas on behalf of the children of the poor, without any reference to the poor or the children themselves. It was time to relocate the mobilisation to poor communities. *"If we take the model of the pyramid, the Alternative Project was an example of power-holders taking one step down from the pinnacle. They discovered us - educators and other programme people - in the middle of the pyramid and they invited our participation. But we were not representative of poor people and we thought it important to involve them. We wanted to turn this pyramid on its head. The co-ordinators of the Alternative Project agreed it was a good idea in principle but kept equivocating over the right moment,"* says Padre Bruno.

Chapter nine

A wider mobilisation of poor community children

The Republic, which had been developing its grassroots nuclei and the representation of children within its own organisation, was highly sensitised to democratic concerns. In Belém a new stage in the participation and organisation of children was taking place.

In the first year of the Alternative Services Project and independently of it, a group was formed by people from different organisations working with children in the city, foreshadowing the other activist groups formed through the Project around the country. It started with the coming together of different church initiatives, including the Republic, to form the Minors' Pastorate in Belém[1]. Those involved were all Catholic but other denominations soon concerned themselves, including those of the Protestant Church and Spiritism movement[2]. For a period in the early '80s, FBESP, the Pará State agency responsible for the welfare of children, came under the leadership of a particularly enlightened president, social worker Mario Barbosa, a follower of Spiritism. He adopted something of the Republic's approach, employing educators to initiate work with children on the streets and, for a while, educators from FBESP and the Republic trained together. FBESP also became involved in the group.

What the members of the Belém group shared was their interest in listening to children and stimulating their participation. Meetings began to be held between children associated with the different organisational members of the

---

[1] The Minors' Pastorate in Belém differed from that in megalopolis of São Paulo. The latter was created to be an assistance programme for children in the streets whereas the former was an articulation of organisations already working with children, and having in common religious faith. Father Bruno was in the co-ordinating committee of the Minors' Pastorate in Belém and subsequently of the National Movement, resulting in a smooth relationship between the organisations in that city, whereas in in some centres there was an element of rivalry.

[2] Spiritism in Brazil is a religious movement deriving from the beliefs of Alain Cardec of France but interwoven with African spiritual beliefs.

Pastorate and then with children from the other programmes in Belém, the MAC, Lar De Maria - part of the Spiritist movement concerned with street children - FBESP and Community Youth Action (AJOC), a movement in Bengui.

Joâo Gomez was a member of the latter organisation. After being a working child in the Republic, he had gone as a part-time volunteer to the City of Emmaus and become active in the local community.

"I was touched strongly by the struggles of the people in this invasion land in Bengui," he says. "Many families had occupied the land. When they held demonstrations, the police would come and beat them up and burn their banners. 'How could such a thing happen?' I asked myself. I had had experience of working with young people and got involved in a local youth movement - AJOC. At first they only prayed together, so I said, 'Let's do something about the poverty here.' We had the idea of starting vegetable gardens for families with working children. People liked the idea but it didn't work out. The important thing was that we started doing educational work, discussing with the children all kinds of issues, developing a critical view of the reality in which they were living. Then we linked up with children in the Republic and others to form a forum of children from different organisations[3]."

This development was to bring a completely new dimension to the participation and organisation of children.

"We were interested in hearing what the children had to say and wanted them to develop a sense of themselves independently of the organisations attending to them," says Padre Bruno. *"We wanted them to understand that, although they were associated with the MAC, the Republic, FBESP, they were much more than that - they were individuals in their own right who shared a common reality. We also wanted to counter the tendency for organisations to regard the children they assist as their children. We can have this same problem within the Republic, with individual animators or educators who come to think of the children they work with as theirs."*

---

[3] Joâo Gomes went on to become involved in the struggle of the residents of Bengui and later became the leader of the aforementioned Commission of Poor Districts of Belém (CBB), as a first step changing his own title from President to Co-ordinator. Under his leadership, the CBB has won many significant victories.

But how did the meetings of children from different organisations differ from those of the grassroots nuclei and the assemblies in the Republic? *"Some of the issues were the same; others were not,"* says Padre Bruno. *"Children from the Republic might also talk about the Republic at these meetings, but less so about its internal affairs. The focus was on things the children had in common - issues related to the family, education, health, violence. Through these discussions they developed a stronger sense of shared life experience and of having a common cause."*

The children of the Republic who took part in the discussions were elected delegates of their grassroots nuclei. Those from other organisations, which had yet to develop children's participation to the same degree, would have volunteered or been selected by adults who worked with them.

Breaking away from the Alternative Services Project

The members of nine NGOs and community organisations consulted by the Alternative Services Project had to meet periodically with the Project team. This gave them a chance of holding parallel discussions among themselves, something that would otherwise been impossible given the travelling costs involved. They were becoming increasingly uncomfortable about acting as advisors to government agencies about what was best for children of poor communities when they had no mandate beyond being representatives of their own projects. They began to talk of forming an independent movement committed to children's rights which would in some way involve children themselves.

A number of the activist groups formed in the bigger cities through the Alternative Services Project began meeting together independently of the Project. Then two regional meetings were held.

In 1984, the year before the military ceded power to civilian government, UNICEF Brazil, in agreement with its government counterparts, staged the First Latin America Meeting for Street Children. It was predominantly a government affair but representatives of 30 groups of educators around Brazil were also invited.

They decided to attend not as participants in the Alternative Services Project but as representatives of their own activist groups and they went with the purpose of meeting independently of the main event to discuss forming a national movement. Its primary goals would be the organisation of children and educators and the mobilisation of poor communities. At about this time Padre Bruno withdrew from the support group of the Alternative Services Project, so as to prepare to establish a more representative basis for action in the new movement. *"We wanted a national movement as an expression of organised civil society which could develop and articulate work with children and adolescents with the aim of changing society for the better,"* says Padre Bruno. *"We wanted to go beyond issues of educational philosophy and methodology to address in an integrated way the underlying causes of society's rejection of poor children. Our struggle was becoming more explicitly one of children's rights."*

The birth of the National Movement of Street Boys and Girls

The work of the Alternative Services Project and the growing network of non-government organisations responding in new ways to street children had progressed thus far without major national exposure. The First Latin America Meeting was widely publicised and also brought the new practitioners into the spotlight. They received many invitations from around the country to speak about their work, some of them, including Padre Bruno, becoming extremely well known.

Their next move was to hold a meeting of the activist groups of educators mobilised through the Alternative Services Project. UNICEF agreed to help them to do so. At the meeting, held in June 1985, they formed the National Movement of Street Boys and Girls, whose aim was to enable educators and the children they worked with to organise into a political force. The meeting was declared the first assembly of the Movement. Already the numbers of activist groups around the country involved in the new Movement had doubled to 60. A provisional national committee of 10 street educators representing the country as five regions (North, North-East, Central-West, South-East and South) was appointed to develop the Movement. This committee in turn elected Padre Bruno as the Movement's first co-ordinator.

It set about drawing up the guidelines and principles of the National Movement, which was officially established a year later. Padre Bruno was elected for a second term - this time for two years - as co-ordinator of the national committee, which was charged with organising a struggle for children's rights. Five lines of action were agreed to:

• the training of educators,

- the organisation of children,
- action against violence to children,
- the development of the movement,
- fund raising.

Padre Bruno is referred to by some people as the founder of the Movement but rejects the tribute, asserting that like most things many people were involved in its making. *"There are moments when what is present in everybody's mind coheres and emerges,"* he says.

The Movement started the work of building its identity as an 'independent expression of the civil society' - independent that is from institutional controls, whether by UNICEF, the government, the church, or political party - identifying with people in poverty and the broad popular struggle for democracy. Padre Bruno was able to secure funds from the Dutch De Waal Foundation. In doing so he put the interest of the National Movement momentarily ahead of that of the Republic, which was itself sorely in need of funds at that time. His reason was that it was even harder to get funding for an initiative that did not provide direct assistance, and in a country dogged by corruption, there should be no shadow of suspicion of members of the co-ordinating committee using their position to benefit their own organisations.

The main work of the National Movement during his period as co-ordinator was building itself up, developing its principles and guidelines, and promoting the organisation of children. In addition to the five regional secretariats, local committees were established in almost every state.

Membership of the Movement

The name, the National Movement of Street Boys and Girls, is something of a misnomer. The Movement was open to educators and children, but not exclusively street children. The name reflects the preoccupation of most organisations at that time with children on the streets - whether they were working, abandoned, or runaway children. But, as educators increasingly began to work also in poor communities with the idea of preventing children going to the streets, the frame of reference widened to include children denied their rights and at risk of becoming marginalised from society. Today, the membership of the National Movement includes schoolchildren from poor communities and adolescents who have left street work through assistance projects like the Formal Work Market of the Republic. As 'street children' became more firmly associated in the media with children abandoned on the streets, as opposed to working, there was some talk of changing the name but by then it was too well established.

After lengthy and difficult debate, it was resolved that the membership of the National Movement should be open to educators as individuals, not as representatives of organisations. Strongly resisted by some organisations, this rule was intended to cut out members jostling for greater decision-making power on the grounds of the size of their organisation and to protect the Movement's independence from both church and state. It also allowed educators to join who were from organisations not necessarily in sympathy with the goals of the movement, such as government departments. While most educators work as paid employees for assistance organisations - government or a non-government - their work for the movement is voluntary. Because of this voluntarism, educators who join the movement are referred to as militants of the movement.

In the early stages, it was necessary to mediate tensions between members of the National Movement employed by government and non-government organisations. There was strong antipathy among the latter towards the state, and the movement vociferously denounced violence against children in state institutions and by the police. Some more sectarian members from the non-government side believed the National Movement should be closed to any government employee. This was obviously tough on progressive members from government institutions, particularly on those who were also penalised by their employers for their involvement in the National Movement.

Such tensions moderated as the National Movement became more confident and clearer about its relationships with the state. Today, people working in state entities represent some 40 per cent of the membership. *"It doesn't matter whether you are employed by a government or non-government organisation,"* says one government-based educator. *"When you join the movement, you identify with its way of seeing things."*

It also took some time to clarify the respective roles of the National Movement and other localised programmes and movements. Most of the children involved in the Movement were involved in government or non-government assistance programmes. Some of these organisations argued that 'their' children should represent them and not the Movement when they were involved in activities related to the Movement. But this was to miss the whole point of the Movement providing the opportunity for the children to take part in a broader political organisation and the chance to develop a sense of independence from a particular assistance programme. Later, the National Movement introduced an associate membership for organisations sharing its commitment to the participation and organisation of children.

Exactly how children should participate in the National Movement was not at first clear. It was felt that it should be left to them to define their own form of involvement.

End of the road for the Alternative Project

The Alternative Services Project continued to operate for about a year after the establishment of the National Movement and then it was closed down by UNICEF. Opinion among senior UNICEF staff at the time as to the reasons for its closure is divided. Bill Myers asserts that the Project had simply served its purpose; he had begun arguing for its termination more than a year before, on the grounds that there had been a levelling off in the formation of new groups. In terms of the emergence of new ideas, says Myers: *"I had the feeling we had seen the main ones. I argued we were carrying on with the programme because UNICEF was making a good name out it, not because it was any longer the best way of spending $200,000 a year. Not only had the project fulfilled its purpose, it was also beginning to compete with its own progeny. Finally, the National Movement itself came and said it couldn't grow while the Alternative Services Project was over its head. John Donohue (UNICEF's new representative at the time) heard that."*

Myers had also argued that the Project would never stimulate sufficient NGOs to constitute an adequate response to the problem of street children. *"I became an anathema for a while to the people I worked with because I said this bottom-up strategy by itself was not enough. We had originally found 70 projects and in time came to know of more than 500. The project was generating a great deal of creativity but you could see it wasn't going to create enough projects of adequate quality to reach enough kids. To reach half the kids out there we would need 25,000 projects of the typical size we had then. There is no way we would get them. The multiplier effect wasn't there. We'd run out of saints. Somehow society was going to have to work in a more systematic way,"* said Myers.

Myers portrays the then Secretary of Social Assistance as being opposed to the idea of NGO assistance programmes displacing government responsibility. He told Myers: *"Our biggest challenge is how to live with the consequences of the Alternative Services Project. If we leave it as it stands, all it's going to do is generate something parallel to government. That will let the government off the hook too easily. It can shove the responsibility on to someone else and won't make the resources and mandate of government available locally. There will be great confusion. We have to accept the challenge the alternatives have given us, and now invent an alternative to the alternatives."*

Children take the initiative:
the making of the First National Meeting of Street Children

In 1985, at a meeting of children from different organisations in Belém, a child from the Republic, Floriana Junio, threw in a suggestion that was momentous in the development of the organisation of children. He proposed that they meet with children in other cities in Brazil to see if their experience was similar to that of children in poor communities in Belém. A letter was composed proposing a national meeting addressed to children around the country via the regional offices of the National Movement.

Benedito dos Santos, then in the National Movement's Central-West Region Committee, describes his surprise on receiving the letter: *"The principle of children having a voice and participating in decision making was a priority of the Movement, but it was not yet developed. So this initiative by the children of Belém posed a powerful challenge to us."*

With the help of the educators, the children of Belém co-ordinated the First National Meeting. They began by choosing the themes to be discussed and sent the list out to children in other organisations. These were the issues most discussed in their own meetings - health, school, family, work, violence and organisation. Groups in different cities selected which subjects they wanted to address and prepared presentations. Delegates were then chosen either by educators or, as in the case of the Republic and the City of Emmaus, by their grassroots nuclei. The children of Belém, met with the leaders of the delegations from the other regions ahead of the meeting to make the final arrangements in Brasilia.

In May 1986, in the first event of its kind, some 500 street and working children - ranging from the most streetwise from São Paulo to the most unworldly from Amazonia - bussed with their educators into Brasilia for the meeting. UNICEF, which was generally supportive of the development of the National Movement, anticipated some public alarm over the thought of so many street children descending on the capital. It held preparatory press briefings, inviting journalists to help correct the public image of socially excluded children. They could help pave the way to more creative public attitudes and policies for street children.

Given the history of children's participation and organisation in Belém, the team from the State of Pará was well prepared for the Brasilia meeting but not many groups had that advantage. *"It was really quite crazy,"* reflects Padre Bruno. *"There had been little time to prepare. We were worried that something would go badly wrong and destroy the purpose of the meeting, or damage the public image of the children. So we were very alert. There was a very delicate moment when the children surrounded the car of the Governor of Brasilia. But generally there were only minor problems of the kind you would expect. The atmosphere was one of gaiety and companionship.*

"What moved me most was the children's speeches. They had not been worked on with the educators. They were spontaneous. The children put their points across in a very fresh, forthright manner of their own. It had a fantastic impact throughout Brazil. It was completely new for children from poor communities to address audiences, give TV, radio and press interviews, speaking confidently about their own life experience. I saw a number of journalists in tears. One said he had never seen a conference taken more seriously by its delegates."

The children condemned the violence they were subject to and their lack of access to basic health conditions, education and housing. The government welfare system of internship operated by FUNABEM and the FEBEMS also stood condemned by the children's accounts of their experiences, validating growing criticism of state welfare policies and reinforcing calls for the scrapping of the Minors' Code.

The children also visited the National Congress. They were amazed by the spacious luxury of the place and kept demanding of the guides: *"What did this cost? What did that cost?"* Despite an injunction to be silent, they entered the 'black room' (a reception room in the Senate) banging percussion instruments and executing *capoeira,* somersaults. *"They invaded the whole space,"* says

Padre Bruno. *"Some senators spoke with them and they asked very forthright questions. One girl asked: 'Is it right that a policeman feels free to rape me?'"*

At the end of the meeting, the children drew up a report of the issues raised under each discussion theme and presented it to the government. The document became a reference point in the subsequent formulation of proposals for a children's clause in the new post-dictatorship constitution. The meeting was the first intervention by children to contribute to the reformulation of law in Brazil, and perhaps anywhere.

It had other important consequences. For the Republic, it was a triumphant expression of its own founding idea of demonstrating the talent and ability of the children society treats as disposable. It was a step towards integrating children from poor communities into the forefront of the struggle for children's rights. Within the National Movement, it promoted the organisation of children from a declaration of intent to a priority practice. Educators and militants in the movement were greatly encouraged by the discovery that children had a strong contribution to make to changing society. National meetings and the preparation for them were to become a feature of the organisation of children within the National Movement - a means by which they could both address policy makers and participate in the development of the Movement itself. After each meeting the National Movement reviews its goals and lines of action.

The First National Meeting also began to make children in cities around the country aware that they too might take action to try to influence events. *"There was a proliferation of local and regional meetings of children in the north-east, in Pará State and in the central region of Brazil, in Cuiabá, Campo Grande, Goiânia,"* recalls Padre Bruno. *"All of a sudden these children became present in a very significant way in all developments concerning children."* In particular they took up the banner against the violence visited upon children with impunity, holding events and demonstrations. After the National Meeting, Children's Day (October 12) as well as May 1 became days of children's mobilisation.

At first, relatively few of the participants in the national meetings were elected by their groups, rather they were chosen by educators. Over time, grassroots nuclei, with elected leaders, became the favoured form of organisation of children within the National Movement. Representatives of grassroots nuclei also began to hold municipal and state level meetings[4].

Antonio Carlos Gomes da Costa, a former manager of public policy who at this time joined UNICEF as its National Project Officer, said of the First National Meeting: *"Society was accustomed to looking at these children exclusively as needy, seeing what they did not have, what they did not know, what they were incapable of - a totally negative profile compared to the middle-class norm. The National Movement presented them in positive light, emphasising what they could do, what they did know, what they could offer the country[5]. This event also reinforced awareness of the emergence of a widespread non-church national movement, a movement well diffused throughout the country with a critical and transforming approach to reality."*

According to Da Costa, the vibrant expression in the nation's capital of the demands of the most rejected members of Brazilian society also had a decisive impact on the policy for children in difficult circumstances of UNICEF-Brazil. UNICEF became a key facilitator of a national social mobilisation for children's rights in the latter half of the '80s and into the 90s. *"The children were the first to raise the issue of violence against children in Brazil and they placed it firmly on the agenda,"* says Gomes da Costa. *"In each of the themes they discussed, it was clear that violence was the common denominator. That is when UNICEF changed the emphasis of its programme for children in especially difficult circumstances. In the first half of the '80s, it had encouraged community alternatives to the state's assistance of street children. From this meeting on, the goal became the prevention and reduction of the violence against children and adolescents."* This change of emphasis resulted in the agency working with partners it had never worked with before, including the police, the Justice Department and human rights groups.

---

[4] The grassroots nuclei of the National Movement are made up of children from different assistance programmes. Some of these programmes also encourage the organisation of children in grassroots groups, as does the Republic. Some of the children from these groups will also participate in nuclei of the National Movement.

[5] *Brazil: the Fight for Childhood in the City*, Anthony Swift, Innocenti Studies, UNICEF, ICDC, Florence 1991.

The beginning of a wider social mobilisation for children's rights

In agreeing, in 1985, the country programme for children for the next four years, UNICEF Brasilia's new Representative, John Donohue, and the government departments it worked with, abandoned the traditional lists of fixed programmes and projects in favour of a goals-oriented approach to social problem solving. As regards street children, the goals were to reduce violence experienced by young people, and help Brazilians protect children more effectively than they had in the past.

Part of the strategy would be greater support for community-based initiatives offering educational, recreational, vocational training and income generating opportunities[6]. But UNICEF argued that, given the varied components - legislation, economic policy, social practices, institutions - which determined what happened to children, the goals could be achieved only if society generally could be galvanised into thinking about them, revising its views about the difficulties experienced by children and seeking solutions. In keeping with the drafting by the UN of the Convention on the Rights of the Child, the focus should be legislative reform guaranteeing children's rights. UNICEF proposed an extensive advocacy programme and mobilisation of civil society in support of children's rights, as well as technical support for institutional reform in the juvenile justice, police and public welfare systems.

---

[6] *Making Democracy Work for Children - UNICEF and Brazil's struggle for Children's Rights*, Barbara Schmidt-Rahmer, UNICEF Brasilia, June 1990.

Chapter ten

The struggle for constitutional rights

Another element that favoured UNICEF's proposal was that, following the end of the military rule, Brazil in 1986 set about redrafting its constitution. Assisted by UNICEF, the government formed the National Committee of the Child and the Constitution. Its purpose was to draw up a draft constitutional clause for children and adolescents. Various ministries were represented and certain non-government organisations were consulted by the committee. State level committees composed of government and non-government members were also formed to produce recommendations.

Widespread publicity in support of the consultative process and constitutional rights for children was achieved through an extensive mobilisation, facilitated by UNICEF, of the media, industry, commerce and professional organisations. In a country that had known two decades of dictatorship, such consultation of organisations of civil society by government was something new and - from the government perspective - a great concession. The National Committee of the Child and the Constitution, however, did not manage to engage broad popular support and its consultative process crumbled towards the end. It completed its brief but for the National Movement the process was too government-dominated and the resulting draft text was far from satisfactory.

For its part, the National Movement was busy at the time establishing its own structure and principles of association. Not all its members were immediately convinced of the relevance of law to people who were poor and oppressed. Justice in Brazil was said, ironically, to be reserved for the poor. The law rarely worked in their interests. Some in the National Movement dismissed the government/UNICEF mobilisation around the constitution as a preoccupation of middle-class institutions. Others argued that there were good reasons for getting involved. Rights could not be so readily demanded if they lacked legal status. Educators often found their work frustrated by children's judges interning children under the Minors' Code and by the violence against children by the police and others. *"We held a national debate which concluded that if we were to defend children within the justice system, we had to secure their rights in the law,"* says Benedito Rodrigues dos Santos, who in 1988 succeeded Padre Bruno as General Co-ordinator of the National Movement. There would also be educational value in joining the mobilisation for children's legal rights. *"In the military period we could not participate in forming public policy. We could only criticise what the authorities were doing,"* says Dos Santos. *"Now that we could begin to participate we had to do more than simply denounce. We had to make our minds up about what it was we wanted. Lobbying for children's rights demanded that we did that. Take education; we were united in the criticism that the need for children to work impaired their chance of an education. But, when it came to how they might be reincorporated into the school, our views differed. Some argued for special schools for street children, others for special classrooms inside the regular schools, and there were people who didn't believe in the formal school at all."*

It would also be educationally valuable to involve children in the struggle for their constitutional rights, the more so as other popular groups - the landless, the women's movement and the black peoples' movement - were also mobilising for the inclusion of rights. Finally, a regulation governing the drafting of the constitution allowed for the submission of amendments from any quarter for which more than 30,000 signatures had been obtained. So there was a real opportunity to contribute to the content of the constitution.

In March 1988, a meeting of NGOs prominent for their concern about the rights of children, was held at the suggestion of Antonio Carlos Gomes da Costa, then UNICEF's National Project Officer. Gomes da Costa was knowledgeable in the workings of government and of the Congress and his advice was greatly valued by non-government activist for children's rights during the struggle for new legislation and after. Key participants in the meeting were the National Movement of Street Boys and Girls and the Minors' Pastorate. They reviewed their progress and decided their weakest areas of action were campaigning against violence and their engagement in the constitution process. Their major quarrel with the perspective of the government Commission for Children and Constitution was that it did not include the marginalised child. *"They thought only about children as being in institutions, or in the family, or school. Children on the streets were not really in focus for them,"* says Dos Santos.

The NGOs resolved to form the National Forum of Non-government Organisations for the Protection of Children and Adolescents (the Forum DCA). Its initial purpose was to mobilise the widespread participation of civil society in formulating a new draft amendment to the constitution to be known as 'Children, a National Priority'.

Broadening the front for children's rights

The Forum DCA was not a new institution but an articulation of individuals and organisations irrespective of religion, race and creed. It drew up a set of principles of association rather than a statute, which smacked too much of an institutional identity. Under these principles each member had a vote in a deliberative and policy making general assembly. Decisions were made by consensus. *"We do together what we can agree to do together,"* as one member put it. It was decided that member organisations would take it in turns to host the Forum DCA; the first to do so being the National Movement of Street Boys and Girls. Benedito Rodrigues dos Santos, the National Movement's co-ordinator, was elected the Forum DCA's first National Secretary.

A fundamental principle was to act in accordance with the Convention of the Rights of Children, then being drawn up by the United Nations, and subsequently with the new Brazilian Constitution. The founding members of the Forum DCA included the National Movement of Street Boys and Girls and the Minors' Pastorate - whose networks of educators and assistance projects were by now widely distributed in Brazil. Other founding members were the National Front for the Defence of Children's Rights (FNDC), and the Association of Ex-students of FUNABEM (ASSEAF), a Rio-based movement of people who as children had been institutionalised by the state.

The Forum DCA aspired to be the main conduit for the views of civil society on children's rights and so did not admit government members. It was prepared to co-operate, however, with both government and other non-government organisations. To avoid being categorised as an instrument of the left and to gain a wider public attention, it set out to broaden its membership. Among those who joined it were some of the professional organisations which had been consulted by the National Committee for the Child and Constitution, including the Brazilian Bar Association (OAB) and the National Association of Paediatricians.

In the same period, forums, fronts and other groups were also being formed around the country to promote children's rights in each state and to work in collaboration with the Forum DCA.

UNICEF decided to extend logistic and material support to the new non-government amendment initiative. In doing so, it endorsed the claim of the non-government organisations to a greater degree of public participation than had at first been offered them by the government. It also provided valuable strategic support and advice and helped in establishing high level contacts in government, business and commerce, who would not normally have collaborated readily with organisations identified with the popular movement.

The Ministry of Education also supported the new advocacy campaign, aiming to secure consensus among non-government and community-based organisations and others. Through the joint action of its members, the Forum DCA did indeed become the main channel for the synthesis and expression of the views of civil society on children's rights. As a result, the pioneers of the most progressive approaches to working with poor community children - who had previously operated on the periphery of Brazilian society - came to the heart of the process of formulating the country's new constitutional rights for children.

A number of commentators regard the Forum DCA at this period as a triumph of solidarity. Lawyer Wanderlino Nogueira Neto, who participated as a consultant in the meetings of its National Secretariat, said: *"It served as a school of political and operational articulation with certain sectors. We have no tradition of this in Brazil, so it was a great school. I have worked in social movements and, in the past, felt that the enemy is all too often the partner at one's side. The progressive forces of the left in Brazil have this anthropophagus characteristic; the enemy is not on the Right, but the person on your Left. So the assemblies of the Forum DCA had precisely this didactic role of creating a new set of practices."*

There was an intense mobilisation of the public and media by NGOs and other organisations of civil society. In urging the adoption of the Child and National Priority amendment, the members of the Forum DCA organised debates at various levels and such events as *cirandas* of the constitution, (circular dances by children), throughout Brazil.

Many educators of the National Movement and the organisations they worked for made good use of the educational opportunity offered by the mobilisation for children's rights. For instance, Dos Santos's project in Goiânia, Youth Village, staged its own constituent assembly. *"We fashioned our organisational norms, using the same mechanisms employed by congressmen. We called it the internal constitution,"* he says.

Suggestions by children went into the melting pot of ideas submitted from many different quarters to the Forum DCA secretariat. There they were collated systematically and passed on to a group writing the constitutional

114

amendment. In some states, children in the National Movement lobbied their congressmen to support the children's amendment and questioned them about violence against children. The degree of participation of poor community children was stronger in some centres than others. The new amendment found widespread public support, gaining 250,000 signatures - well ahead of the number of signatures supporting the *Child and the Constitution* amendment - as well as an additional 1.4-million signatures of children which, though they had no legal status, packed moral punch.

On the rival amendments being presented to the Constitutional Assembly, the *rapporteur* proposed that they should be fused. The amendment supported by the greater number of signatures, *Children, a National Priority,* was taken as the basic text and additional elements in the other text were incorporated.

In May 1988, immediately before the vote on the Chapter for Children's Rights, another mass advertising and media campaign was unleashed. A giant *ciranda* was danced by children around the National Congress.

Children get constitutional rights

Chapter VII of the Constitution (on the Family, the Minor and the Aged) and the inclusion of Article 227, which guarantees the rights of children and adolescents, were approved with a resounding majority of 435 to eight.

The new constitutional provisions for children and adolescents incorporate the principle of full protection - family, society and the state are required to protect children and adolescents as a matter of absolute priority. They are guaranteed rights to life, adequate food, a family, leisure, education, occupational training, employment rights, culture, dignity, respect, freedom, social security. They are to be protected from all forms of negligence, discrimination, exploitation, violence, cruelty and oppression.

The discredited legal definition of poor community, abandoned and delinquent children and adolescents as being in irregular circumstances is discarded. Instead, all children are due special protection as people in a process of development.

The NGOs had wanted to import the entire text of the draft UN Convention on the Rights of the Child into the Brazilian constitution, an ambition defeated on grounds of length. Instead, in the introduction they encapsulated each right symbolically by a single word. Effectively Brazil adopted the Convention even before its approval by the UN General Assembly[1].

The new Brazilian Constitution was promulgated on 5 October 1988. A major feature was the emphasis on the devolution of power and responsibilities from central to state government and state government to the country's 5,000 municipalities. Crucially, allowance was made for organised civil society to be directly involved in designing, executing and monitoring of social policies.

The victory of the constitutional amendment for children owed much to the particular historical moment - that of a population rooting for democracy after two decades of dictatorship. The struggle for children's rights - and for children to also have a say - chimed strongly with the struggle of people in general for rights and became a banner of that struggle. Furthermore, the drafting of the UN Convention on Children's Rights occurred at the very time in which Brazil sought reintegration into the 'democratic' world. Embracing the Convention was an opportune means to signal to that world the country's new direction. The argument, advanced by UNICEF, which strongly appealed to the politicians was that Brazil had the chance to be the first country to ratify the Convention.

But there was little commensurate political commitment to effect the structural changes needed to guarantee children's rights, as was reflected in the assembly's failure to make constitutional provision for land reform. Protagonists for children's rights knew all too well that, without land reform, a key cause of poverty went unaddressed and the displacement of poor people to the cities and of poor children to the streets would not be stemmed. The mere declaration of rights was not enough. Means were needed to ensure that they would be respected.

Changing the framework for the struggle for children's rights

The constitution victory achieved, the members of the Forum DCA - which was still hosted by the National Movement of Street Boys and Girls - turned immediately to drafting proposed enabling legislation to replace the Minors' Code; without that, children's constitutional rights would remain in the realm of good intentions.

---

[1]A study of the constitution reveals that the only rights not included relate to refugees of which there are very few in Brazil.

Another proposal for a Statute of the Rights of the Child, was being developed by the Public Prosecutors of Sâo Paulo, with whom the Forum DCA had worked closely during the constitutional phase. They decided to join forces. The resulting text was delivered to the National Congress within months of the promulgation of the constitution. There was a strategic advantage to lodging a proposed text before other contenders and there was a fear that supporters of the Minors' Code might submit rival draft legislation. Public consultation and changes would be possible as the legislation progressed through the Congress.

Forum DCA had further broadened its alliances, which now included among others the National Council of Education Secretaries and the Brazilian Association of Toy Manufacturers. These and other organisations provided material support, advisory services and technical and legal assistance and co-sponsorship of debates and events. The National Advertising Council, which had also supported the constitutional process, now recruited publicists and communicators and allocated free television and air time in support of the Statute. Famous individuals - artists, actors, musicians and sports figures - came out in favour of the Statute and helped to popularise the issues. Journalists wrote articles describing the experiences of children and progressive ways of working with them. UNICEF again played a key role in mobilising support.

The Forum DCA staged a number of major seminars including the First Judicial/Parliamentary Meeting on Justice for Children and Youth. It also participated in the XIII Brazilian Congress of Juvenile Court Judges and Trustees. The draft legislation was widely distributed for comment by the members of the Forum DCA, supporters, and the state-level forums for the rights of children. Meetings, seminars, study groups and conferences were held throughout the country.

As part of the participatory process, the Forum DCA organised an open seminar in Brasilia to discuss the initial draft. It was attended by people from government and non-government organisations and institutions and the draft was sharply criticised as being still too reminiscent of the Minors' Code and failing to express adequately the new spirit of the constitutional amendment. The message, says one commentator, was clear - the lawyers responsible for the draft were still too much in the sway of the legal paradigm that had prevailed for the past 50 years. More play had to be given to the views of the popular movement[2].

A writing group was formed, composed of a variety of people - militants in the popular movement, priests, educators, social workers, law makers and experts from different disciplines. A welter of suggestions from the public flowed to the secretariat of the Forum DCA, where it was collated and passed on to the writers. The criterion for the inclusion of suggestions in the draft law was the Whole Protection Doctrine of the United Nations which underpins the Convention and the Declaration of the Rights of Children.

Some 10 versions were produced, each being fed back for further comment and revision. In the spirit of the new democratic times, the leadership in the drafting process is said to have come from the non-jurists, with the legal experts facilitating. Though the draft legislation was the product of a wide range of people, it gave expression to many of the ideas of the activists and militants who had pioneered the new approaches to socially abandoned children.

It is said that there never was a law composed with so great a public participation. Some activists describe it enthusiastically as a democratisation of law-making procedure, expressing the powerful democratic aspiration of the time.

Padre Bruno believes this to be true in a limited way. *"The mobilisation was probably as extensive as it could have been at the time, but it was still much more one of the middle than the popular classes - technical and professional people, experts from different government institutions, children assisted by these organisations, movements that were specifically focused on the needy children,"* he says. *"Residents' associations, the families who benefited from the assistance organisations, community centres, grassroots communities, women's organisations, agricultural communities in the interior - these real popular segments of society were not generally involved. The unions were also absent."*

Through the educators of the National Movement and the Minors' Pastorate and others, however, the debate did reach and yield responses from some poor communities as well as organised groups of children in some 120 of Brazil's 5,000 municipalities.

---

[2]*Making Democracy Work for Children - UNICEF and Brazil's struggle for Children's Right*, Barbara Schmidt-Rahmer, UNICEF Brasilia June 1990.

The Forum DCA also sustained a lobby of congress during the progress of the Statute. Through its member organisations it mobilised mass telegram campaigns to politicians at crucial moments, and made a point of attending and intervening in all the major meetings of its opponents. Tough opposition was anticipated from the children's judges. But by now the issue of severely deprived children was no longer the concern of a tiny minority of activists. The mobilisation for children's rights had caught the imagination of a wide range of Brazilians and gained a momentum of its own with many different organisations and individuals contributing spontaneously to the process.

Even senior officials in parliament would tip off Forum DCA lobbyists about important moments in the passage of the legislation to which they should attend. *"Instead of being regarded as defenders of thieves and robbers, we were becoming respectable,"* comments Mario Volpi, who became the third Co-ordinator of the National Movement. Children's rights were firmly on the political agenda.

The solidarity of some prominent individuals and organisations carried great weight in the National Assembly, among them Dom Luciano Mendes de Almeida of the CNBB, Padre Bruno, the OAB, the Association of Heads of Public Institutions (FEBEMS), the Service for Justice Against Violence.

Among the many imaginative events in the mobilisation for the Statute, one of the most prominent was the Second National Meeting of Street Boys and Girls staged in Brasilia in September 1989.

The Second National Meeting of Street Children

Since the First Meeting, the National Movement had been developing the participation and organisation of children. Many 'integration' activities - meetings, and recreational events bringing children from different programmes together - had been devised around the country. As a result, a more thorough preparation was possible for the Second Meeting. Themes were discussed by children in the grassroots nuclei and other groups. In some states delegates from groups in different municipalities held state-level conferences, which in turn selected delegates to participate in the national meeting.

Some 700 children of the National Movement attended. This time, on visiting the National Assembly, they occupied the Congress itself. Some congressmen had agreed to receive a delegation but the children arrived late.

119

"We had gone to demand approval of the Statute of the Rights of the Child and Adolescent," recalls Maria de Nazaré Costa, then a child in the Formal Work Market of the Republic and in a nucleus of the National Movement in Belém. *"They said they couldn't see us so we staged a demonstration outside, demanding our rights as Brazilian citizens and displaying many posters and banners. Then we all went together and invaded their space. It was our own initiative. The police tried to bar our way but we were too strong for them. We sat down in the chairs in the Congress and held up our posters and some of us began to speak from the platform about the Statute. Those who spoke did OK. They talked about all the problems we were facing. It was very good. I think the congressmen were taken by surprise, but they were also impressed. We were able to tell them everything we wanted to."* Congressmen gave up their seats to the children.

Violence - in particular the killing of children by 'death squads' composed of policeman, businessmen and others - was a major theme of the Second National Meeting. The children held a symbolic vote in favour of the Statute and denounced the killings, which were the subject of a joint report by the Rio de Janeiro-based action/research NGO committed to the democratisation of information and of society, IBASE, and the National Movement[3].

On the last day of the meeting, the children unfurled a banner bearing the names of children known to have died. They released a white balloon for each victim. Their exposure of the killing of children initiated media coverage which ultimately forced the government to take serious action to try to combat it[4].

Children involved in the National Movement and other organisations, including the Minors' Pastorate took part in many other events, demonstrations, marches in different parts of the country.

---

[3]*Children and Adolescents in Brazil: Lives in Peril*, The Brasilian Institute of Social and Economic Analysis and the National Streechildren's Movement, 1989.
[4]Gilberto Dimenstein's book, *Brazil: war on children*, researched with the help of the National Movment was important in exposing the killing of children.

Maria's story:
From the periphery of Belém to the Second National Meeting

For a child of 10, working at the São Brás market can be very scary. But for Maria de Nazaré, Costa taking food home was 'a sacred activity'. *"My father was a security guard. He earned very little. My work provided my family with the daily meal,"* she said.

Maria assisted a woman who sold vegetables. At first one of her sisters worked with her but found the going too tough. Children were regarded as pests by some stallholders and subjected to exploitation and abuse by others. Girls suffered endless sexual harassment from men.

"You had to be very closed in on yourself, because they put a lot of pressure on you," says Maria. *"At times the stallholders would even chase us out of the market, or seize our merchandise. They would beat up the paper bag sellers. They were really mean. It was hard to earn enough by selling vegetables. Some girls did sell their bodies to get a little money for their families. At times I didn't want to go to the market, but I had no choice. I was lucky, I had only one real problem with one stallholder and the animators from the Republic helped me to deal with that.*

"They came one day and introduced themselves to us and told us about the Republic of the Small Vendors. I told them about this man who was worrying me and they listened very carefully to me. They invited me to visit the Republic. We went there for lunch and met up with many other working boys and girls. Some girls were even smaller than me. We could go there at weekends, as well. There was lots of recreation, games to play and excursions into the countryside. We would also discuss our problems in the work place, or at home, problems with drugs, sexuality, violence against children. We felt these educators were really interested in our well being. They gave us a lot of strength to find our way and deal with our lives. It was a very good experience.

"In the Republic I began to speak in other groups as well as my own. I found that when I opened up about myself, other children would also begin to talk. Even if you couldn't solve a problem, it was very good to be able to talk about it with the others."

When she turned 16, Maria was chosen by her grassroots nucleus to join the Formal Work Market and work in the federal bank. *"We were given training in the Republic and the bank people gave us lots of attention and the educators were always following up on our work,"* says Maria. *"I was elected by the adolescents from the Republic to represent them. Departmental heads would come to me if there were problems and we would discuss these problems at the Republic on Saturdays. These were usually small problems related to the fact that the children were not so used to discipline.*

"However, we also tried to negotiate a pay rise - we were getting only half a minimum wage. We didn't succeed at that time. We also tried to get the uniforms changed. The material was very thick and hot. We wanted to wear shirts and jeans. We didn't win that one either.

"Then I was elected to represent the employees' group at the Second National Meeting in Brasilia. We discussed all the issues in our groups - about children rights, about violence - and we took these ideas to Brasilia. A congressman paid for the bus and there were other children with us from Castanhal and Santarem. It was very good to see all the other children from all the other states and to exchange information with them. There was a lot of joy and enthusiasm.

"I took part in the discussions about the Statute and violence. I was very shocked to learn of the killing of children in São Paulo, Rio and Recife. When we came back to Belém we told other street and working children what had happened. At school, my teacher and principal asked me to tell my class why I had been away. When I finished they said this work with street children was very good."

Note: Soon after the Second National Meeting, Maria turned 18 and so left the Republic. She got a job in Belém as office assistant with the National Movement's Committee for the Northern Region and continued with her schooling. Her plan is to become a lawyer and work for the street children's cause.

The Statute for the Child and Adolescent - a law for a better future

The Children's and Adolescent's Act was adopted by the National Congress in July 1990 with the unanimous support of the leaders of all parties. For those organisations which had been fighting for the cause of excluded children for many years it was a momentous victory.

The legal context of people working with poor community children was radically changed, creating important new possibilities for the participation and organisation of children. The Act's opponents have disparaged it as a law for first world conditions, or as utopian.

"They say they want a law based on Brazilian reality, but how could we who work in a practical way with children legitimate the misery, poverty and insecurity in which they are made to live?" asks Benedito dos Santos. *"In our projects with children, we are working with them towards a better future and have to anticipate that future. Well the law was also a project, and there was no way we could legalise children going out to work at the age of eight or nine, for instance. So we said children should work only after 14 years of age, and today some people accuse us of having a law that doesn't relate to reality. If we had made a law that mirrored reality, it would have justified hunger, misery, poverty."*

The Act defines three categories of policy:

* Basic Social Policies assure all children of the right to health, care, education, job training, and other basic services;
* Social Assistance Policies establish the minimum level of well-being calculated to preserve the dignity of needy children and their families;
* Special Protection Policies are for victimised children, including those with disabilities, the homeless, children in institutions, orphans, and victims of drug addiction, discrimination, negligence, exploitation, abuse and police or institutional violence.

The Act does more than anticipate a more humane future; it provides new instruments to empower those ready to struggle for it[5].

Policy and programme development are decentralised to municipalities and states. A radical innovation is the establishment of Municipal, State and National Councils for the Rights of Children and Adolescents, which give non-government organisations concerned for children a direct say in policy making. Composed equally of government appointees and elected

---

[5]The brief outline of the Statute that follows draws on *Brazil: A new concept of Childhood,* Irene Rizzini et al., *Urban Children in Distress, Global Predicaments and Innovative Strategies,* Cristina Szanton Blanc with contributors UNICEF 1994.

representatives of organisations of civil society, their job is both to make and monitor policy; promote and monitor programmes designed to guarantee the rights of children and eliminate the many weaknesses and waste in welfare provision[6].

The implementation of policies at all levels is to be achieved through co-ordinated governmental and non-governmental action. NGOs concerned with child-related issues are required to register with their Municipal Child Rights Council to gain access to public financing, a measure designed to avoid overlapping programmes and gaps in service provision.

The Act substitutes the principle of controlling children in 'irregular situations' with that of guaranteeing their rights[7]. FUNABEM - the central agency responsible for such children under the old law - is scrapped. The Brazilian Centre for Childhood and Adolescence (CBIA)[8], which replaces it is more streamlined, its role confined to establishing policy guidelines and co-ordinating implementation of the Statute at the national level.

Policies for children in need of protection are administered through a new Guardianship System operated by front-line Tutelary Councils and social services. Each municipality creates a number of Tutelary Councils proport-ionate to its child population and the district it covers.

Though paid by the municipality, Tutelary Councillors are elected by the community they serve and so answerable to it. Tutelary Councils take over many of the decision making powers previously allocated to children's judges. They are of particular interest to educators and others working directly with children. Councillors must be well integrated into the communities they serve and experienced in working with children. Their role is to ensure that children in need or at risk receive the best possible assistance. They also handle all cases of offenders under 12 years old,

---

[6]The role of the state-level councils is to support their municipal-level counterparts in planning and evaluating programmes, developing human resources, undertaking research, and implementing programmes beyond the scope of individual municipalities.

[7] It meets the standards set down by the United Nations Convention on the Rights of the Child, the Standard Minimum Rules for the Administration of Juvenile Justice (the Beijing Rules), the Guidelines for the Prevention of Juvenile Delinquency (the Riyadh Guidelines), and the Rules for the Protection of Juveniles Deprived of their Liberty.

[8]Antonio Gomes da Costa moved from UNICEF to become President of the CBIA. During his Presidency he put the agency's weight behind the development of children's rights and combating violence against children by the police.

working closely with the families. Anyone - children themselves, families, teachers, social workers, policemen or other officials - may ask a Tutelary Council to intervene. The council is the point of entry into the service system and is the link between children and families in need of assistance and government and non-government services. Tutelary Councils both interact with, and complement, the rest of the service system and advise municipal governments on budgets and plans of action. Their work is likely to produce a much clearer definition of the circumstances of socially marginalised children in Brazil than has yet been available.

Guardian, foster and adoption placements of orphaned, abused or abandoned children are still referred to juvenile courts, along with adolescents aged 12-18 accused of committing an offence. The latter gain the right to due process of law. Sentencing ranges at the judges' discretion from admonishment to deprivation of liberty, but its aim must be to strengthen young people's ties with their families and communities, and promote their personal development and social integration.

The Act imposes new protective conditions on the processing of children suspected of offences. New integrated screening centres are established, co-ordinating police, judiciary and social-welfare responses to suspected child offenders and ensuring that children pass through the justice system as quickly as possible and that their legal rights are respected. The juvenile courts, together with the Public Prosecutor and the Tutelary Council, also monitor governmental and non-governmental institutions to ensure that standards are met. The mobilisation of different sectors of the community is envisaged to support families, society and the State in guaranteeing children's rights.

The Republic during the struggle for the Statute

In addition to the changes in constitutional and federal law, state constitutions and municipal laws were redrafted. Organisations committed to children's rights also engaged in this process, working through state non-government forums and other alliances in many centres to unify their demands and actions.

Like other organisations and movements, the Republic participated in various ways. It was represented on the Forum DCA through the Children's Defence Centre (CDM). Educators from the Republic were active as militants in the northern regional Commission of the National Movement of Street Boys and Girls. They encouraged debate and collected signatures in

125

support of the mobilisation for children's rights and organised local meetings and events. Children from the Republic went with others to demonstrate outside the Pará State Congress in support of the Statute. Animators and volunteers at the City of Emmaus stimulated debate and concern in Bengui and the Campaign of Emmaus promoted children's rights themes in its annual big donations. The Republic was able to make good use of its access to the media, built up over the years, to promote the debate on children's rights. Violence was a major preoccupation of the children's movement. Late one night a group of older children drew graffiti profiles of assassination victims on the roads and walls in the Ver-o-Pêso district. Such action was being taken by children and educators in a number of cities.

Chapter eleven

The struggle for the citizenship of the child in daily life

While the legal rights struggle was being waged, the struggle to change public attitudes and establish the citizenship of the child in the social reality of the slums and streets continued to be prosecuted with increasing difficulty. Deepening poverty engendered ever greater levels of social insecurity and violence. There was an increasing exploitation of children by criminal gangs, who used them as look-outs, to gain entry to buildings and to deliver drugs around the cities. In various centres, among them São Paulo, Rio and Recife, the killing of children with impunity by death squads reached chronic proportions. Some educators working in the tougher urban districts could name dozens of children known to them personally who had been killed.

Conditions in Belém also deteriorated. The city was spared the phenomena of death squads, but both children and animators confronted growing levels of violence. Nara, who began working with children in a poor community in 1985 and joined the Republic at the end of the decade, provides a glimpse of what animators had to contend with: *"One night we came across policemen who had five children up against the high wall of the colonial fort (Forte do Castelo). This was before the Statute was promulgated. They were beating them, hitting them particularly on the genitals. I told them to stop it. A policeman shouted at me, 'Shut your mouth or I'll shut you up'. I was furious. I told him, 'OK, so beat me up. I want to see it.' People were gathering, demanding to know what was happening. The policeman accused me of defending marginals and criminals. I said the children had done nothing but sniff glue. While we were arguing the boys made a run for it. The next day they came up to me in the street to thank me. I was very moved. After that I always intervened when I saw violence."*

Drugs were also more commonplace by now, complicating the work. One day Nara came across a boy in convulsions on the pavement. In the busy street, people were stepping past him. A girl in a very drugged state was with him. She explained he had taken a drugs cocktail and it was affecting his heart and breathing. *"They called it boogie-woogie,"* recalls Nara. *"I asked the girl what to do and she said I should massage his heart. So I cradled his head in my lap and massaged his heart and he came round. He became a good friend. I liked him very much. But he took an overdose when he was 18."*

The Ver-o-Pêso team of animators in the latter part of the '80s - Maria dos Reis, Dino and Lucia Gomes - found themselves working in a situation permeated by conflict.   Children were no longer following particular occupations as in the past, so that the basis for organising them was weakened. Some nuclei were now formed around dealing with conflict.

At the same time, prior to the promulgation of the Statute, clear victories against violence or other abuse by state officials were rare. At one point the municipality was restructuring the market area and placing it under tighter management.   A raised platform was erected in the middle of the fish market to give security personnel a commanding view. *"If they saw a child fighting or misbehaving they would impose some punishment,"* says Lucia. *"They made children wash out the toilets or do rigorous physical workouts in a closed area of the market. We spoke to the managers and won some concessions from them but in return they said they held us responsible for the behaviour of the children. That was the kind of deal we might strike."*

The animators also had increasing problems with Military Policemen (PM)[1] who sometimes accompanied the *rapa*. The Military Police had a small cupboard in a caravan parked close to the commercial centre - referred to as the PM Box - in which they temporarily held children they arrested. The animators would have to go to the PM Box to argue for their release. *"The* rapa *would beat the children and take their merchandise, and we would have to intervene,"* said Maria. *"Sometimes there was a lot of aggression. With the Military Police there too, we would sometimes find ourselves surrounded by these two hostile forces. On other occasions it was calmer and there was more chance to discuss the situation with them."*   The animators urged the children to call them if they saw any child being beaten or arrested.

They also strove to improve the attitudes of market stall holders towards child hawkers, talking to them individually, occasionally holding small meetings, appealing to class consciousness and respect for the right of all people to participate in the struggle for survival. *"Even the market people*

---

[1] Despite the name, the Military Police in Brazil police civil society. Their structure and training is military and they remained a closed institution into the '90s. Both they and the Civil Police, who carry out investigations, have powers of arrest.

had begun to think of the children as criminals but we succeeded - for a while - in getting them to regard them as workers again," says Dino. The animators also tried to tackle the abusiveness of fish sellers towards young girls on the streets. *"They were terrible,"* says Maria. *"We had to be very firm and courageous to face them and open a dialogue with them. I think they did begin to see us differently. We developed a relationship with the manager of the market. We were a reference in the market, even for children who had no opportunity to become involved in the Republic. The vendors, the security guards, everyone knew us. Generally, no-one was violent towards the children when we were around."*

Contending with violence on the streets - verbal and physical - was like contending with a tide. It ebbed and flowed. At one point competition for trading space broke out between fish and vegetable sellers. *"It was a case of people condemned to a life of misery fighting among themselves. Inevitably the children would get embroiled,"* recalls Maria. The animators worked as best they could to unify the different factions and, where successful, encourage the children to act in solidarity.

Plans to reorganise the Ver-o-Pêso area triggered a major action by the children in the grassroots nucleus. Some adults were being moved out of the area and the children feared they would be next. With the animators' help the children in the Ver-o-Pêso nuclei prepared a case to put to the State Secretary for Economic Affairs, whose office was responsible for the restructuring and in charge of the *rapa*. They elected representatives from among themselves to go with the animators to put their case to the secretary at a formal hearing. They also got other children who worked in the central area to attend the hearing.

"They went there with handfuls of bags and their trays of merchandise. There were around 200 children in this assembly," recalls Maria. The hearing was attended by the Secretary, a representative from Public Security and the *rapa*.

The animators had made some inquiries and found there was some sympathy for the children within the City Hall. *"So we knew this was an opportunity for discussion,"* recalls Lucia. *"We didn't go in a confrontational mood but to find ways to deal the situation. The children who took the proposal started to raise such issues as the violence of the* rapa *and confiscation of their merchandise. The* rapa *were very angry but they didn't say much because the children had hard facts. A child would say, 'You did such-and-such to me on that day. I remember you confiscating my goods - you threw them away and you beat me up.' And the guy would say, 'No, no, not me - I would never do that'.*

"The Secretary gave the children's representatives a big welcome. He was very diplomatic. He told them he regarded their allegations seriously and would take action. It was not the job of the rapa *to beat children or hamper their efforts to survive. Of course he was a politician and only posturing; he knew very well what went on. Then the children demanded a discussion with the* rapa. *That took place at another time, with the animators. Two or three children who were the leaders did the talking and some other children also gave witness."*

As usual after such initiatives, pressure from the *rapa* eased a bit for a while. Fearing possible reprisals against children who had spoken out, the animators intensified their presence on the streets and made a point of trying to build better relationships with individual members of the *rapa.* *"We perfectly understood the process the* rapa *was part of,"* says Maria. *"The city authorities made decisions about people's lives without their participation and, of course, that resulted in conflict. And the* rapa *were deployed as a confrontation force. They came from the same poor districts of the city as the dissatisfied people they were deployed to suppress. They were in the middle, between the people who made decisions and those denied a say in decision making. So we started to work away at them. But the moment the people from the Commerce Secretariat realised they were softening they would move them to another district and we would have to begin all over again."*

In another incident, Padre Bruno recalls some children forming their own commission to talk with some Military Police who had treated them violently. The children waited at an appointed place, and two soldiers walked hesitantly towards them but at the last moment turned and strolled away again.

At another time the municipality decided to control the numbers of children working on the street. It wanted to introduce a standard stall for use by child hawkers. Badges would be issued, a selection made from among the children and a register kept of those permitted to work. The authorities looked to the Republic for its collaboration, promising that none of 'its' children would be penalised. Some children in the grassroots nuclei were interested. It would end their problems with the *rapa*. The scheme, however, would also exclude many children, who also had to earn a living.

"We went through a whole reflection with the group about why many children from poor families had to work and had to be able to work. The Ver-o-Pêso nucleus came to see that the scheme would create a privileged group of working children and exclude and damage many others. It was one of those moments when the spirit of solidarity surfaced again," says Maria. *"The group decided against the Republic supporting the plan and eventually the authorities abandoned it. How could they restrict people who were simply trying to survive, when national political and economic policy was condemning them to unemployment and poverty? It was unthinkable!"*

Such victories were pinpricks in the system but milestones in the development of the consciousness of the children and animators involved. The Republic scored some other notable victories in the latter half of the '80s.

The Republic's Formal Work Market doubled its potential to provide work experience by entering into an agreement with the Electricity Company of Pará State (SELP). The agreement was at first not so favourable. *"Somehow we failed to examine it closely and so signed for an eight-hour day[2]. The long hours undermined the children's schooling,"* recalls animator Lucia Gomes. The oversight, however, had a valuable consequence. *"Meetings were held to discuss the issue and a commission of children was elected to work with the animators in drafting a new agreement to put to the company management. We redrafted the original agreement in terms the children could understand. This time they were also directly involved in the negotiations with the company. There was a whole educational process involved."* Having to negotiate with children was not the only surprise in store for the company. The representatives of the Republic on this issue were women and lay people.

"They never expected that," recalls Georgina. *"We had to tell them that this matter was now our responsibility and not Padre Bruno's. It wasn't easy, but they ended up accepting it."*

---

[2] This kind of apparent lapse of attention is hard for outsiders to understand. It is a mark of the extreme pressures and lack of resources people working directly with poverty are subject to, as well as the turnover of membership in the movement. There are moments when those engaged in the movement are collectively clearer about what they are doing than at others. Strivers though they are after perfection, they are also the first to advise outsiders that if it is perfection they looking for they would best look elsewhere. *"Don't expect anything to be perfect,"* I was warned.

Important concessions were gained, including a four-hour working day, a minimum wage rate and guaranteed workers' rights.

The loss of community experiences

A major defeat of the '80s was the collapse of the community experiences which had been at the heart of the Republic and its associated expressions. They had enabled the participants to have fun together, to reflect together and work more consistently on the kinds of relationships they would like to see operating in society at large.

They came to an end in 1987. The immediate cause was that the Republic faced financial difficulties. Coincidentally, there were security problems at the donated house occupied by the Children's Defence Centre (CDM) in another part of the city. Reinforcing it against break-ins would be costly but if the CDM moved to the Republic the house could be let, solving both problems. The CDM relocated to the double-storey wooden house at the Republic that had been used for community living.

The community experiences, however, would not have been sacrificed so easily were they not already undermined by the movement's earlier decision to remain within the Salesian fold and therefore answerable to the congregation. Key members of the Republic who were then on the brink of making a life commitment to the Republic and forming a permanent community had abandoned the idea. Georgina had got married - settling for nuclear family life on the rebound, she says, from the loss of the communal option occasioned by the Republic's decision not to claim its autonomy. She continued to be activist in the Bengui, where she lives, and stayed on in the movement for a few more years, working at the school at the City of Emmaus, but the closing of the community option remained a matter of regret. Though also an activist, her husband has other areas of interest than the Republic.

Ironically, a decision taken by Padre Bruno at this phase of the Republic's development unintentionally precipitated a break with the Salesians. He had become increasingly worried that he had allowed the Republic to become over-identified with him, both as an individual and priest.

He had become very well known. *"Even today too many people think that the Republic is Padre Bruno. I should have stood down as general co-ordinator long ago,"* he says. In fact such a move would have been

132

difficult, given the movement's status as a Salesian initiative in which a Salesian had to remain in charge.

"There was a powerful tendency for people to vest the values we tried to practice in Padre Bruno," agrees Georgina. *"As if only a priest were capable of such a commitment. This traditional attitude was evident when we lay-people approached enterprises for support. Doors that would open immediately to Padre Bruno were more impenetrable for us, though we were on an identical mission."* Similarly, if people wanted someone to speak about the movement, it was Padre Bruno they insisted on hearing.

Public attribution of the movement to the work of a rare charismatic individual might have appealed to popular Catholic mythology but it confounded the crucial message of the movement - that the life choice it represented was that of ordinary Brazilian citizens and so was available to society in general. Even within the movement, the deeply ingrained tendency to relegate moral action and social responsibility to the preserve of the priest was not easily overcome. Georgina was twice elected co-ordinator of the Republic - in 1983-84 and 1986-87. *"Some people who disagreed with a decision of the co-ordinating committee in those periods would say, 'Well, I am going to go and sort that out with Padre Bruno', as though he would override the elected co-ordinating committee,"* she recalls.

Padre Bruno leaves the Republic

In 1989, Padre Bruno decided to break off his association with the Republic for a period. He withdrew from the Salesian congregation for two years for what was intended to be a period of reflection.

A year earlier, just ahead of the mobilisation for the Statute, he had also resisted various requests to stand again as National Co-ordinator of the National Movement of Street Boys and Girls. He stayed on, however, as Co-ordinator of the National Movement's Commission for the Northern Region. He had several reasons for not standing again. One was his conviction that people who speak for the oppressed should not stray far from them. Another was his preference for working at the grassroots level to ensure the participation of the people most excluded from social decision-making processes. Finally, he was determined not to make the mistake with the National Movement that he had made with the Republic. A national movement for children's rights ought not to become over-identified with or over-reliant upon one or even a few individuals. In a participatory

133

democracy, leadership, and the skills and qualities it allows people to develop, should be shared.

In mid-1989 Padre Bruno went to live in a slum house in a poor community and took on the role of Co-ordinator of the Social Pastorates. He also travelled throughout Amazonia on behalf of the National Movement's Committee for the North, setting up a network of children's rights activist groups. At this time, most of the work on children's rights had been undertaken in the country's major cities. It was time to extend it to the interior. Despite Amazonia's exposure on the environmental front, it remained and still remains the dark heart of Brazil as far as human rights are concerned.

Members of the Republic are not very forthcoming about the two-year period of Padre Bruno's absence. It is almost as though there is a collective amnesia about it. He was replaced by another Salesian. Clearly the arrangement did not work well and there was a weakening both in the spirit of the Republic and in its educational work with the children. In particular there was a loss of emphasis on the very aspect of work with children that the Republic had pioneered - their organisation.

In fact, there were other more complex reasons for this latter development. The triumphs of the grassroots nuclei in the mid-to-late '80s marked the completion of one of the cycles that characterise a movement involving children and youth. The leaders of the nuclei had for the most part moved on out of the Republic by the end of the '80s. Most of the animators involved in that process had also gone elsewhere, or taken up other posts within the movement. *"We were going into a dip,"* says one of the animators. Among those who left ahead of Padre Bruno's departure were Ana Sgrott from the school in the City of Emmaus, Maria and Dino. They went to work for the National Movement's Commission for the North, with Ana as co-ordinator. Lucia and Nara had moved to the POA as animators.

"The priest who replaced Padre Bruno was a manager rather than a religious orientation person," says Georgina. *"The spirit of the movement was lost in some measure. I can remember him complaining to me, for instance, that my working as a volunteer was inconvenient and inefficient."*

Georgina was in fact at that stage still working within the volunteering tradition of the movement - earning her living by teaching part of the day in a conventional school. She left the movement in 1992 with some sense of disappointment.

A momentous outcome of Padre Bruno's two-year period away from the Republic was the decision by the assembly, shortly after his return, to break from the Salesian congregation. *"I know that I had to go away when I did. I think it did help the Republic to gain recognition in its own right, independently of me,"* says Padre Bruno. The break with the Salesian congregation was not what he had sought or expected, although he accepted it as inevitable.

At the election the following year Padre Bruno stood down as General Co-ordinator and stood instead for election as co-ordinator of the CDM. The Salesian congregation agreed to release him to undertake the work.

The Movement of the Republic of Emmaus

In 1992, the Republic, the Campaign of Emmaus, the City of Emmaus and the CDM set about rewriting their constitution. After much discussion, they decided to call themselves the Movement of the Republic of Emmaus, recognising the key points of reference. Each component of the movement retains its autonomy, holding its own policy making annual assembly and having its own elected co-ordinating committee. Three categories of membership of the movement are defined - affective, collaborative and affiliated. Affective members are well wishers, volunteers and employees who have a special commitment to the movement. Collaborative members are the employees. Affiliated members are the children. Overall policy is reviewed and made at an annual assembly, attended by the co-ordinating committees of the different expressions, as well as representatives of the three membership categories of the movement, including the children. Co-ordinating committees of the expressions are elected for two-year terms of office and are represented on the movement's Executive Council. A new administration and services secretariat - the SAG - was created.

At the assembly of January 1992, the movement elected its first co-ordinating committee and a lay Co-ordinator General, Bido Francisco, who had had experience in the Campaign and the Training Nuclei.

Tougher going in '90s

Without internal problems, the movement would have found the going hard in the worsening economic blizzard of the early '90s. On the streets and in poor communities, the situation of children was deteriorating as the 'lost decade' of the '80s gave way to the insecure '90s of continuing international recession, privatisation, downsizing and the 'free-market' licensing of self- rather than social-interest. With the nation's wealth still concentrated in the

135

hands of a small minority, in such a climate the advent of western-style democracy brought no material consolations for the poor. There was a decline in the popular movement in general. Corruption at the highest levels cast doubt on the very future of Brazil's infant democracy, deepening if possible public disgust with politicians.

In deteriorating social circumstances, public attitudes towards children on the streets hardened, eroding gains made by activists in the late '80s. Organising children became more difficult, as organisations were pushed on to more of an emergency assistance footing. To make matters worse, aid-funding fashions began to move on from street children to other focuses, leaving many organisations both challenged by the multiplicity of demands upon them and facing a cash crisis.

Excluding its animators and teachers, who were paid for by the government, the number of people employed by the Movement of the Republic of Emmaus had crept up to 57. The increase in numbers of employees partly reflected the general decline in people's ability to work in any sustained way on a voluntary basis as they struggled to hold down two or three jobs to makes ends meet. Idealistically, the movement had set the wages it paid its employees at twice the market rate. *"It's not that we pay good salaries - it's that other people pay very badly. We would be paying $200 a month instead of $100,"* commented a member of the movement.

Inevitably, the shift from a movement based on mainly voluntary action to one which relied increasingly on paid staff introduced a degree of ambiguity, with some members - including some children - alleging that others were involved purely for the job. It also incurred increased administration costs. An associated problem was that expansion of the movement diluted the contribution of people with a deeper insight into its nature, some of whom were both older and more tired and having to spread themselves more thinly.

Graça, for instance, while trying to act as co-ordinator of the School of the City of Emmaus, was also attending increasingly to problems and developments in the Republic. The vigilance needed to sustain the quality of the school's educational practice was impaired. The general erosion of voluntary energy, combined with a sudden turnover of teachers at the school resulted in a deterioration of practice - both in sustaining the Montessori approach and in maintaining links with the community. An associated development was a breakdown of collaboration between the School and Production School.

The school's resources were also being overwhelmed by the number of children in Bengui clamouring for places. Caught in the conflict between responding to an overwhelming local demand and preserving an educational model, the school stretched its capacity to the limit, further undermining its practice.

While the movement's costs had grown, its sources of income were now under attack. In Belém, as elsewhere, middle class people were increasingly taking themselves into protective custody, moving out of traditional houses and into well-guarded tower blocks. In a climate of increasing social insecurity, public attitudes towards children on the streets hardened, eroding the gains of the previous decade's mobilisation for children's rights. *"The situation with our children is a terrible tragedy,"* observed one woman, exhibiting the two-way tug between compassion and self-preservation. *"The killing of children by death squads is appalling. I really feel for these children. At the same time I am very scared of them. They commit so many robberies. My own brother was assaulted recently. Today we go out expecting to be assaulted. And these children have knives and guns. We must protect ourselves. We should go back to the practice of putting them into institutions for their sakes and for ours."*

"We are a population scared of its own children," says Padre Bruno. *"This is a terrible distortion of social relations. We are becoming an imprisoned society, locking up people who have nothing and then locking ourselves up in fortress homes. With this system we are making life impossible."*

The obsession with security was affecting the Campaign of Emmaus. *"Security men in the flats will not allow the volunteers from the Republic in to collect donations, so there is less access to goods from the middle class. The quality of the donations is declining,"* said Rolando Maneschy.

Though still a major event in the town, the Campaign had peaked as an income earner. It continued to be self-funding but it was not a major source of income to the movement. The pressure was on the Production Unit at the City of Emmaus to make a greater contribution to the movement - particularly by supplying food to the restaurant in the Republic. The unit sought the advice of experts on how to maximise income. It abandoned traditional methods of rearing pork and chicken and went in for more intensive production. Meanwhile inflation - rising to 50 percent a month - rapidly ate into the value of foreign project grants gained by the movement and government funding alike.

Deterioration on the streets

On the streets the situation was becoming more complex, demanding new strategies. The number of children on the streets was growing and among them were much younger children, a sign of growing poverty. *"We used to have children from ten-to-twelve years up,"* said Graça. *"Now we are getting them as young as five or six. At fourteen, children can come to understand that street life is no good for them in the long run and that they have to do something about it, but there is no basis for awareness raising or organising with a ten-year- old, let alone a six-year-old. So an additional stage of work is now needed that will provide very young children with emotional and moral support until they are able to grasp their predicament."*

The challenge was not only adapting the work to younger children but, with diminishing resources, finding a way to work with children and adolescents across a wide age range. Complicating matters was a growing presence on the streets of young girls and, for the first time in Belém, concentrations of abandoned or runaway children appeared, suggesting a new degree of desperation, distortion and fragmentation in families. Educators found it impossible to integrate street children (those who lived on the streets with little or no contact with their families, surviving on a mix of casual work, begging, prostitution and opportunistic crime) and working children. The latter generally wanted nothing to do with the former. Work with street children had become further bedevilled by a high prevalence of drug taking and glue sniffing.

The Republic's restaurants in Ver-o-Pêso and São Brás became over-burdened - the former running three sittings of 30 children a day. Adding to the confusion was an increasing number of organisations trying to work with street children, which had been encouraged by the national mobilisation for children's rights and the consequent flow of funding from the aid industry in the late '80s.

Some of them promoted dependency and opportunism in the children. *"One of the problems we faced was that other organisations, including the government welfare agency FBESP, were now also offering food,"* says Bido Francisco, then co-ordinator of the Republic's Training Nucleus. *"So the children would choose where to lunch on a particular day. They would turn up at the extension in Ver-o-Pêso just for food; they wouldn't stay for other activities. The picture became very unfavourable for organising children. We had a new situation on our hands.* [3]

Adding yet a further complication at the beginning of the '90s was a graffiti gang craze that swept Brazil. Formed by working and school children, the gangs conducted raids into each others' neighbourhoods, spoiling their opponents' graffiti and marking the territory with their own - usually in such provocatively inaccessible places as the undersides of bridges, or the parapet walls of houses, advertising their daring. The gangs started in the suburbs but the rivalry was also played out in Ver-o-Pêso and São Brás. *"Graffiti gangs began to appear in 1990,"* said Nara, who had begun working in Ver-o-Pêso a year before. *"Almost all the children in Ver-o-Pêso were members of one gang or another. Rivalry and fights became commonplace."* There were also clashes between graffiti gangs and street children who were not involved in the craze. The graffiti gangs preceded the appearance of heavy criminal gangs operating in the districts.

The graffiti craze was seen as symptomatic of a more general infection of American cultural values. Emblems from American films and TV programmes were rapidly translated from TV screens to the city's walls. It became fashionable among the young to wear patched and torn jeans and let their hair grow. There was a hunger for foreign products, stimulated by the Collor government's lowering of tariff barriers. Educators found themselves working in a more distracting era of powerful and insistent commercial appeals to the young, glorifying all the paraphernalia of competitive consumer societies - material possessions, fashion crazes, sensationalism and violence. Questioned about the graffiti craze, the children answered in ways suggesting a social identity more dislocated from the adult world. *"This is what being a young person is about,"* one child would say. *"I don't know, I am going there because I was invited and I am not going to be left out,"* said another.

Gangs began to turn up at the Republic's restaurants seeking out boys belonging to rival groups. Fights broke out. *"We were worried that a child might get killed,"* said Nara. Finally, a boy was killed in a clash in a city park. The restaurants were badly overcrowded and no longer serving their

---

[3] Since the mobilisation for the Statute, government agencies had been adapting their work with children on the streets, introducing many of the techniques of the non-government pioneers. Superficially, there is not much to distinguish certain government-run programmes from those of the NGOs, though there are often profound philosophical and political differences.

purpose; furthermore their rents, moving in step with inflation, became too expensive. The decision was taken to close them. The educators reverted to working on the squares but the troubles followed them there. At one point they had to bar a particular group of children from taking part in their activities, though they remained in contact through their families in the district they came from.

Television, which was becoming omnipresent, was yet another powerful distraction from the work of the educators. *"We got rid of the dictatorship and now there were more subtle commercial instruments of oppression,"* observes Graça, of the more distracting environment in which educators now had to work. *"The government no longer put the army on the streets to silence you. They put TV Globo[4] in your house and now we all sit watching adverts and soap operas. Children won't sit and talk with you in a room when they can watch TV. It was clear that we had to find new ways to attract and hold their interest, and for that we turned to the arts."*

---

[4] Globo prospered during the dictatorship to become by far the country's most powerful television network. In 1992, Globo's programmes were beamed to 96 percent of Brazil's cities, reaching an audience of more than 60-million viewers and 99.9 percent of all television sets. It is accused of using its power to make and break presidents and is regarded with strong antipathy by the popular movement who see it as responsible for the narrow defeat of Lula in his bid for the presidency in 1989. For an account of Globo see the chapter *Globo Village*, by Robert Mader, in *Channels of Resistance - Global television and local empowerment*, Ed. Tony Dowmunt, British Film Institute Publishing, London 1993.

Chapter twelve

Forward with the Movement of the Republic of Emmaus!

Having been the weakest front of the popular movement at the beginning of the '80s, a decade later the movement for children's rights was among the strongest. The women's movement had peaked in the middle of the decade, though the movement of women sex-workers was to gain in strength in the '90s. With the country's move towards multi-party democracy, poor community residents' associations were exposed to division and political manipulation. Landless workers had been set back in their struggle to get agrarian reform into the new constitution, though they, too, were to make a strong come-back. Labour unions were under attack from growing unemployment and changing labour practice.

Organisations concerned about socially discarded children embarked upon the '90s, elated with the victory of the Children's Act. The National Movement of Street Boys and Girls now had the means to represent its interests in a growing number of towns and cities and at state and national levels. Through the Forum DCA, and associated state and municipal forums, it and other organisations, such as the Pastorate of the Minor of the Catholic Church and a growing movement of Children's Rights Legal Defence Centres, were able to broaden their social alliances and lobby more effectively in the interests of poor children.

Among the immediate challenges facing them was that of ensuring the implementation of the Children's Act. The first task was the establishment of the National, State and Municipal Councils for the Rights of Children and Adolescents. Only after a Rights Council was established in a given municipality could the front-line Tutelary Councils, which dealt with the cases of specific children, be set up. Until both types of council were operational there was little change in what happened to children. Because Rights Councils institutionalise the involvement of civil society in policy, however, making, they encroach on the decision making power of mayors and on political patronage, which is endemic in Brazil. As a result, the implementation of the Children's Act was resisted in many centres, not only by mayors but also by

141

certain judges, as well as sections of the police and state and national governments.

Some mayors refused to establish the new Councils unless their wives chaired them. Others created bogus non-government organisations which then sought representation on the Councils. Some municipal authorities appointed junior representatives to the Councils who lacked any decision making authority in their departments. There were policemen who refused to act even when a child committed a criminal offence on the street in front of their eyes. Instead they demonstratively blamed the Children's Act for robbing them of their powers to intervene. Equally, there were cases of policemen who continued to round up children in defiance of the new law.

Opponents of the Children's Act demanded its revision, on the basis that it protected thieves and bandits. In short, champions of children's rights, in government and out, faced a protracted battle for the implementation of the Act.[1]

There was another reason why the establishment of the new Councils could not be instantaneous. Precisely because of their participatory nature, they can only really succeed when they are the product of a demand from a civil society determined to be involved in defining social policy for children. In a good number of Brazil's 5,000 municipalities, there were not even any non-government organisations concerned about children's rights and there was no such demand. Many municipalities were in thrall to political dynasties that had long controlled local political life. If the new Councils were to do more than rubber-stamp mayoral policy in such centres, preliminary work was needed to mobilise public opinion and action around children's rights. In particular in most rural areas - where half of Brazil's millions[2] of working children live and endure conditions even more abusive and dangerous than their counterparts in the cities[3] - there was little organised support for

---

[1] In particular, the Ministry of Justice and the CBIA, which for a period came under the leadership of Antonio Carlos Gomes da Costa, as well as UNICEF and numerous individuals, even within some police forces, fought strongly for implementation.

[2] Estimates of the number of working children vary widely depending on definitions and sources.

[3] For an excellent account of the oppression of rural workers, including children, in Brazil see *Slavery in Brazil: A link in the chain of modernisation*, by Alison Sutton, Anti-Slavery International, London.

children's rights. The network of children's rights activists developed throughout Amazonia by Padre Bruno for the Northern Committee of the National Movement of Street Boys and Girls in his time away from the Republic was a notable early attempt to begin to address the problem.

Even where there was a strong lobby of children's rights activists, as well as support from the authorities for the new Act, much had to be learned on all sides about how to work together. Activists had to shift from purely denouncing government to working with government. They had to learn to translate the lessons derived from their work with a relatively small number of children into public policy proposals[4].

They also had to establish a unified front were they to win policy points in equally balanced Councils where government appointees might strategically vote together. Here their national, municipal and state Forums for the Defence of Children and Adolescents established in the mobilisation for the Statute found a new lease of life. Not all non-government councillors were equally committed, however, and some were largely interested in promoting their own organisations and interests - and in some cities there was rivalry between the National Movement and the Minors' Pastorate.

Faced with the demands associated with the implementation of the Act, some educators in the National Movement of Street Children wanted to abandon the task to others. The struggle for legal rights, they felt, had diverted them for far too long from developing the participation and organisation of children and their own role as educators. Other educators, fearful of a plot by the government to co-opt them as a cheap means of executing social policy, argued that they should abandon all assistance work with children and concentrate their energies on pressuring the government to meet its responsibilities.

In the aftermath of the national mobilisation to secure children's legal rights, the language and practice of the state with regard to marginalised children had changed significantly in many centres. The rounding up, chaining and incarceration of children was officially at an end. State welfare institutions now employed more street educators, created drop-in centres and began to offer

---

[4]The training of councillors become a priority and is being provided by such organisations as the National Movement of Street Boys and Girls and Minors' Pastorate, with some financial or consultancy support on the government side from the CBIA (the successor to FUNABEM) as well as from UNICEF.

occupational training. At a federal level and in some states, the authorities even began denouncing the killing of children by death squads and others. In the view of activists in the National Movement, however, despite the transfer of language and techniques, there was still little evidence of any transfer of the underlying philosophy.

"In Belém, for instance the authorities have backed off from the principle of organising children," said Padre Bruno. *"I do not believe underlying attitudes have changed that much. For the state to wholeheartedly embrace our philosophy (of education for participatory democracy) would be for it to begin working for its own eradication."*

The Movement of the Republic of Emmaus believed it was still important to work on all fronts in an integrated way. *"It is no longer enough to devote ourselves to work on the streets,"* said Padre Bruno, answering those educators who wanted to leave the implementation of the Children's Act to others. *"What we haven't yet achieved, simply by our work, is to translate our experience into public policies which might serve to universalise new social attitudes. Unless we find a way to do that we will remain islands. We have to see where we can get to with the Children's Act. We must sit at a table and negotiate with these (government) people if we are to build a participatory democracy."*

But progressive organisations working with children had to take care not to confuse themselves with the state. There was a danger that the Rights Councils could degenerate into new instruments of top-down decision making - with the representatives of non-government organisations closeted with government in making policy for people condemned to lives of poverty without any mandate from them. The new challenge for the elected representatives of civil society was to establish such a mandate. The greatest achievement of the Children's Act, in the view of many activists, was exactly that the NGOs had been able to establish in law the possibility of grassroots participation in policy making. But they now had to work to ensure that that possibility was realised and that meant taking understanding of the new Act to the poor classes and stimulating their concern for the rights of children. The participation and organisation of children had a key role to play in this work and the great majority of Brazilian street and working children had yet to become involved. It was crucial to continue working with children in order to be able to extend their organisation.

The forums now also had an important role in establishing a mandate from the underclass. They ought actively to encourage representation and demands for accountability from people in poor communities.

Furthermore, another level of organisation was envisaged by the Children's Act, that of grassroots community level Committees for the Defence of Children's Rights. The front line Tutelary Councils would have an interest in their development. Given their limited resources, the scale of their task and the fact they are answerable to a community electorate, Tutelary Councils would need to stimulate all the support they could get from the communities where they work.

"Real change will not come just because the state is good," said Padre Bruno. *"It will not come from the negotiations and handouts of the dominant classes. This is not to deny that the institutions who believe in summit work (such as UN agencies) have a role to play. But, if the mobilisation for the Statute had been left to their way of organising alone, we would have a law made only by those at the top, and one at a great remove from the majority of people. I don't want to deny the merit of that kind of negotiation, but our strategy in the popular movement is different. We put our faith in the strength of our organisation. The pressure must come from the social base, from the growth in people's consciousness that the state must serve and be accountable to its citizens rather than citizens be in servitude to the state. Only then, will things be able to take a different path."*

The situation in Belém

In Pará, the state government dragged its feet in implementing the Children's Act, despite pressure from the National Movement, the Movement of the Republic of Emmaus and others. When the State and Municipal Councils were finally established, the Movement of the Republic of Emmaus was represented on both. Bido Francisco, the General Co-ordinator of the Movement of the Republic of Emmaus, was on the State Council, with the General Secretary, Edmar Holanda, his understudy. Padre Bruno became Vice-President of the Municipal Council, with Nara standing in for him in his absence, and several educators from the Republic were elected to the Tutelary Councils. The movement was also active in the non-government State Forum and nationally represented on the Forum DCA.

The Councils in Belém were recently established at the time of the research for this book and little progress had been made beyond mapping the needs of children and resources for them in the city and sorting out the budgetary arrangements.

Whereas governments traditionally manipulated social spending to secure political goals, the representatives of civil society were determined to fight for an integrated, child-centred programme that would assure children of their rights to health, education and recreation and provide back-up services, including foster home and other arrangements for children at risk, such as those addicted to alcohol and drugs and children on the streets. They also planned to demand income support for families whose children were obliged to work at the cost of attending school. The NGOs believed that some of their goals could be achieved by adapting existing facilities rather than spending huge sums of money on new buildings.

In committing itself to the implementation of the Children's Act, the Movement of the Republic of Emmaus expected it to be 10 years before its effectiveness might be assessed. *"We are already feeling the burden of this new work and we are more fortunate than most organisations,"* said Padre Bruno. *"Because of our size we can spread the load among ourselves and we have a range of specialist knowledge. Even so we will be looking out for early signs to encourage us to continue."*

Arts educators - meeting the new challenges on the streets

Meanwhile, parallel to its involvement in the implementation of the Children's Act, the Republic had another pressing priority in the early '90s - finding a way of working with the broader age range children coming on to the streets, notably the younger children, as well as the growing numbers of street as opposed to working children. It was time to adapt its practice again to the ever changing reality in which it works.

The use of the arts - creative games, drama, painting, dance and circus skills - had been pioneered in other centres, most notably in São Paulo, where the problem of runaway and abandoned children appeared at an earlier stage. The first attempt to deploy them in Belém was made within the Social Pastorates, while Padre Bruno was co-ordinator there during his time away from the Movement of the Republic of Emmaus.

Ever concerned about broadening social responsibility, he at first hoped to get the archdiocese to support an extensive programme of artists working together with educators in the city, but no funding could be found. The Republic decided to go it alone.

Stella Menezes, of the social work department of the University of Belém, who had helped train the previous generation of educators, now assisted in the selection and preparation of arts educators. As in the past, candidates were recruited from young people from poor communities, most of whom had previously worked voluntarily with children in their own districts and parishes.

"We needed to find people with special aptitude, not just of good will. They would have to be spontaneous and playful but also psychologically and physically resilient," says Stella. In its characteristic way, the Republic gathered together an advisory team of artists, theatre people and psychologists, as well as teachers from the Popular University, to devise a training programme for activists in the popular movement (UNIPOP). An art school and a new educators' training centre started in Belém by the National Movement of Street Boys and Girls[5] were also involved. They helped design a two-month training-selection workshop for arts educators in the Training Centre of the Republic and a one-month observation phase in the streets held in mid-1992.

Of 120 applicants, 17 of those who stayed the three-month course were successful. Arts educators are salaried staff, their wages paid under an agreement with the state Education Secretariat, but they carry forward the volunteering spirit.

Street theatre

The arts and education programme started with a bang. *"We had to capture the children's attention,"* says Patricia Cordeiro, a new educator and team co-ordinator. *"We chose the theatre because it employs all the arts and we rehearsed and staged a play in Republic Square. We had some help from drama people. They wrote a short script about the underwear of the king. We simplified it and ended up calling it The King is Naked.*

---

[5]The National Movement began to establish educators' training centres in the early '90s, the first in São Paulo, a second in Belém and a third in Recife.

It was great because Collor[6] was President. With his jet skis and his clothes, he was someone who craved luxury which was a typical aspect of Brazil. He was a kind of king. So, even without our intending it, the analogy was there. We learned how to use our voices, we wrote songs and made the scenery from waste materials. The king was naked, and we gave him a great plastic penis.

"We'd put on our make-up, go into the streets and tell every child we met that the play was about to begin. Sometimes we took puppets and addressed the children through them, inviting them to the play. At the end of the show one of us would thank everyone and say we were not a theatre group. We belonged to the Republic of Small Vendors and were there to work with children who lived or worked on the streets. If there were any in the audience, we wanted to talk to them. Then they would gather round. We would let them touch the costumes and the scenery and manipulate the puppets. Usually people screamed at them, 'Don't touch!', so they loved it. We would arrange to meet them in the square the next day and organise games and playful activities. We generally avoided using lots of materials, relying mainly on our bodies and our voices, so the children could join in.

"These were children who had had their childhood stripped away from them. On the streets people would come to exploit them, or put them into an institution, or give them food, or tell them they should pray to God. No one came to play with them. Yet they are children and they love to play!"

The play was staged in several city squares. Within a month, the arts educators had 50 children to work with. Taking part in dance, movement and theatrical activities on the streets had greater appeal to street than working children, who were more self-conscious and conventional. It also attracted the more extrovert educators, so there was a self-selection process. Three teams of educators were formed. Two teams attended to working children during the day - one at São Brás and the other at Ver-o-Pêso. The other worked at night with street children in São Brás, near the bus terminal.

---

[6]Fernando Collor de Mello was elected President in 1989 on an anti-corruption ticket. With the help of TV stations owned by the elite, he narrowly defeated Lula, the favoured candidate of the popular movement. Though professedly a supporter of children's rights, he had a wealthy playboy image and by 1992 was facing charges of corruption on a massive scale. The popular movement rallied to press for his impeachment. In what was seen to be a crucial victory in the thrust of the popular movement for democracy, he resigned just ahead of being impeached and was stripped of political rights for eight years.

A day in the work of arts educators

Twenty-five years after the first youth group discovered children on the streets of Belém, a team of four young educators gathers in the early mornings in the square opposite the Church of Sé, five minutes' walk from the commercial centre. Like their predecessors, they are in their late teens or early twenties. Although from poor backgrounds, they also attend either high school or university. All want a different society from the one they have had to grow up in and are prepared to invest energy in the struggle for it, whether they stay on in the Republic or go elsewhere.

In other parts of the city at the time of their morning meeting, other vastly more powerful and cynical forces daily marshal their energies to add to accumulations of wealth and protect them from the claims of the poor. But, though the educators still represent a minority, they are no longer an isolated handful of individuals; most have a keen sense of themselves as part of the broadening alliance of workers, landless people and minority groups who compose the popular movement. There is also considerable respect for their work within the city.

Twice a week the team is joined by psychologist Cláudia Macêdo, and social worker Socorro Lacerda, from the Republic, who advise them in their work. Before they plunge into the frenzy of the commercial area, they review the day past and plan the day ahead. Once a week they hold a more thoroughgoing evaluation of their work with Graça Trapasso, now Co-ordinator of the Republic, or Iolanda, her deputy.

Their discussion touches on the arrivals and absences of particular children in the commercial district. There are always incidents to follow up on. On a given day, a boy came to the market - not for the first time - bleeding and badly bruised, the victim of family violence; a girl was stabbed with a broken bottle by another girl, fortunately without serious injury; a fight broke out between two boys in the restaurant at the Republic; and a boy, bound by a rope, was seen being led through the streets by a mounted policeman in blatant contravention of the new law. The educators intervened promptly to stop the fight in the restaurant. It had started with a new boy boasting that he had tricked the cook out of an extra plate of food. He offered to share it but then set about a younger boy at the table who objected that that was no way to treat the Republic.

The educators consider how best to resolve such conflicts so that the protagonists gain some understanding of their aggression and can set it aside. They may speak to each child separately and then together, and possibly raise the incident for discussion in the group. In the case of a battered child, an educator will visit the family, accompanied by the psychologist and social worker.

Like their predecessors, the educators intervene whenever they encounter violence. But they now have the law on their side. They go armed with pocket-sized versions of the Children's Act to show offenders against children's rights that they are contravening the law; not infallible protection, but it helps, whether they are tackling a school principal trying to exclude a child from school or a policeman maltreating a child. Where police officers refuse to observe the law when challenged, the matter is referred to the Movement of the Republic of Emmaus's Children's Legal Defence Centre (CDM).

The educators also discuss the daily activities they organise with the children during the lunch period. These are a lively mixture of educational and socialising games, discussions, workshops, recreation, sports and lunch. In keeping with the principle of the child as the subject of his/her own development, the agenda is developed around issues raised in discussion by the children themselves and drawn up in agreement with them. *"Our planning is bottom-up,"* says Elias Santos, co-ordinator of the Ver-o-Pêso team. Workshops usually have a direct bearing on the children's lives. They may focus on an aspect of their work, a particular occasion such as Children's Day, or Mother's or Father's Day, a health theme, or a provision of the Children's Act.

Street and working children in such programmes are often better versed than other children about their rights. *"It is very natural for us to talk with these children about the law governing their rights,"* says Elias Santos. *"It bears directly on things that happen to them every day and to rights they do not yet have. They get beaten, they are neglected and out of school, and now it is the duty of parents, society and the state to ensure these things don't happen."*

The children are also encouraged to participate in cultural and religious social events - such as the widely observed St John's Party, Labour Day, or Christmas. They explore and discuss the cultural origins of such festivals, learn folkloric dances associated with them, prepare costumes and decorations, present theatrical or dance performances and join the processions. For instance, a dance group of children from Bengui community, many of them from the school at the City of Emmaus, performed traditional dances at an annual meeting of the city's neighbourhood associations.

The educators review the successes and failures of their activities. The children had begun arriving from the streets to take part in activities in such an excitable state that they could settle to nothing. The educators had tried relaxation sessions. A few older boys had refused to join in and mocked the others for doing so. Given the option of going or staying, on condition that they respected the right of the others to take part undisturbed, all chose to stay. During the sessions, however, one displayed a strong aversion to being touched. Perhaps he had been abused? Cláudia, the psychologist, explains that there could be various explanations. The boy might even have complicated sexual feelings for the educators themselves. They resolve to pay him closer attention. In discussing disruptive children in the group, Amarilda Marinho speaks of one who exercised great patience in teaching a new eight-year-old girl volley ball. The educators decide to try giving the more disruptive boys more responsibility.

Going to the area

Their meeting over, they go to 'the area', the commercial district incorporating the downtown shopping area and the richly supplied fish, fruit and vegetable and meat markets of Ver-o-Pêso on a bank of the Amazon estuary. On the way they pass the small scruffy caravan of the Military Police containing the 'PM box', where children were still sometimes illegally detained.

The commercial district is a clamour of bright colours and cheap goods, aggressive traffic and pavements congested with hawkers and shoppers. From doorway loudspeakers, pedestrians are assailed by loud music and urgent appeals to step in and buy. They are often deluged in turns by torrential rain and tropical sun. Close to the equator, Belém has the highest rainfall in Brazil, often resulting in humidity that stifles each act of exertion. Heavily polluted by traffic, the district also has a reputation for muggings and assaults, even in broad daylight. On Flávia Chagas's first day as an educator she confronted a young gangster, reputed to have killed several people. *"He wanted to beat up a boy in the group. I wouldn't let him,"* she said. *"He stared at me, testing me. I was very scared but stood my ground. I had to be very cool and sure of myself. I and another educator told him this was not the moment to fight with this boy.*

We persuaded him to leave. Luckily he left Belém altogether soon after that. He was getting too well known."

The team works intensively with some 30 children, ranging from six years' old to 16, but is in touch with many more. *"We have worked as educators for two years. Some of our colleagues have already moved on to other things. More will soon follow. After our training in arts and education, seven of us were assigned to this area in two teams. Now, two years later, we are four. At this point the Republic has no money to broaden its activities,"* says Elias Santos[7].

The arts-education experiment is up for review and only after that will new educators be trained. The Republic is considering proposing to the Municipal Children's Rights Council that a city-wide arts education programme should be launched.

Most of the children in the group Elias works with, sell something - herbs, bags and snacks. There are many others who do not join the Republic's activities, usually because they cannot afford the time out of their working day. To respond adequately to the needs of all the children in the district would require more educators working with a variety of approaches and with referral opportunities that currently do not exist. The social will to tackle the problem on that scale is not yet established.

Wearing Movement of the Republic of Emmaus T-shirts, the educators are a presence in the district. Stall holders, shopkeepers and police know them, at least by sight. Not all are supportive. The three young women in the team contend with jibes from men in the fish market. The team's progress through the market is overlooked by security officials who are fond of neither them nor the children. Stall-holders sometimes make a grab at the girls or throw fish debris at them as they pass. The good will won by previous educators has again been eroded. A number of stall-holders, however, do respect them and one or two are quick to speak and act in their defence. A meat market trader is full of praise: *"These people from Emmaus do wonderful work. Many children who would be in prison have gone on to get jobs, thanks to them,"* he says.

---

[7]Such was the Republic's financial crisis at this time that it had only enough money in the bank to fund its activities for a further two months and with no expectation of imminent income. It was having to consider cutting back its activities. Padre Bruno was undismayed, anticipating that something would turn up. The movement's accountant complained: *"There is still a tendency here to rely on Divine Providence. But its a tough line to sell to the bank manager."*

As the educators work their way through the crowds, they greet and are greeted by children and youths. Because the children are working, the educators do not detain them in lengthy conversation. Smaller children snuggle up to them, eager to snatch a welcoming hug, and often walk along hand in hand with them for a while before vanishing back into the crowd. Some older ones are more guarded in public, offering gruff and fleeting salutations. At each encounter a few words are exchanged. How are they? What is happening? Are they coming to the activities? This walkabout is about being available to the children in their environment and on their terms, listening to any problems, keeping informed and taking action where necessary. It is also about letting the adults in the area know that the children are not on their own.

The youngest child discovered unattended on the streets by the educators was three years old. A boy from the group took them to her. They found the tiny girl, in a rag of a dress and with unkempt hair, reaching shyly up to passers-by begging for food. She told them her twin brother was somewhere about but she did not know where. Later they learned the mother was also in the area. They tracked them down in different parts of the commercial district. The mother, though carefully dressed and made up, was totally disoriented, as though she has lost all ability to cope with life. The three were taken to Cláudia and Socorro at the Republic, to try to work out some solution.

At midday, the educators and children meet at a bus stop to go out to the Republic. The journey is expensive and unsatisfactory, the ride hot and crowded. Passengers often complain that the children are noisy and smell of fish. Travel tokens provided by the Republic are an expense it can ill afford. When they started working on the streets, the arts educators held recreational activities in a square in the city centre but, as the children demanded more than just physical activities, and given the climatic extremes in Belém, some kind of premises became essential and there was nothing available near the centre. Travel concessions had been sought from the bus company and the City Hall without success.

Activities at the Republic

With Mother's Day approaching, the children have been exploring ideas of what it is to be a mother and the extreme difficulties facing mothers in poor communities. As a basis for discussion about the role of mothers in the family and community, the educators asked them to say whatever came into their heads when they thought of their mothers. They also invited them to compare different images of motherhood, including those portrayed on television and through advertising. Part of the purpose was to reinforce the children's understanding and respect for their mothers and for their own origins.

In a related workshop project, they learned to make artificial scented roses. Such flowers are popular in Brazil, where fresh cut flowers are a luxury. Each child wanted to make a flower for his or her own mother as well as some to sell. To do so, they had to identify in discussion the different aspects of the task - the raw materials they would need, how to work together, how to cost the venture, price and sell the flowers and distribute the profit among themselves. As part of daily activities, the educators chose games which stimulated manual dexterity, including origami. Apart from the children's acquisition of new skills and sense of their own creativity, the educational values pursued were, as always with the Republic, social - the experience of belonging and co-operation, individual and group achievement, taking responsibility and a working through of concepts of fairness, self interest, the needs of others and sharing.

Group activities are held in an airy meeting room, brightened up in the case of Mother's Day by the colourful roses the children had been making. Chairs with writing pads attached to one arm allow for flexible use of the space. For discussions, children and educators usually sit in a circle on the floor. Anyone who stays demonstratively outside the circle is coaxed to join in. If a child wanders off - as one did to inspect the flowers, peering critically into each and delicately removing a speck of dust - no one shouts at him to rejoin the group and he returns in his own time. The educators also take in their stride occasional bouts of boisterousness - ragging and joking, running around and even trying to climb the walls. The children soon settle down again. In a conventional classroom, such behaviour would meet with punishment or expulsion. But the educators in the Republic are not trying to control the children. They want them to act responsibly out of concern and respect for others. Their trump card is that no child is compelled to attend; they choose to. The worst sanction is to be reminded that they may also choose to leave. The appeal to mutual respect is basic in the Republic, and it tells strongly with children who, in lacking everything, lack nothing so much as respect. Despite bouts of skirmishing and testing behaviour, most want very much to participate in the sessions.

Asked what they value most about the Republic, the younger children say, *"the friendliness of the educators"*, *"the warmth"*, *"the touch"*, *"being together"*;

whilst older ones say *"the discussion"*, *"the work we do with the educators"*, *"making the flowers"* and *"voting"* - participating in the decision making.

The arts educators are the main point of access to the Republic for children on the streets. A number of children go on from their groups into the more formal educational activities of the POA and the Formal Work Market, where educators who have had street experience as well as instructors follow them up. A number also continue at regular school or go back to school, who otherwise would have left. The educators visit the children's families to explain their work and engage family support. They also seek parental support for the children's formal education and access to the opportunities offered by the Formal Market and the POA. Where there is a choice to be made between school and attending the activities of the Republic, they insist that school takes priority. They would like to strengthen the work with the families but, as in the past, lack of resources makes it hard to be consistent. About a third of the children the educators work with currently attend school. They would like to see the number greatly increased.

Some children do not get beyond the street-based group and remain essentially as street workers but they do gain an experience of being loved, valued and respected as well as some social and other skills.

Daily activities are followed by lunch in the Republic's restaurant. The meals are generous, varied, inviting and nourishing and dished up to educator, employee and children alike. After lunch, the children play soccer or a variety of other games. They then take a cooling shower and set off back to work in the downtown area, or to school or home.

The educators also go off in the mid-afternoon, either to study or work. Often they do additional voluntary work for the Republic; for instance, helping prepare for the annual Campaign or with special projects like constructing a new music and arts and dance room in one of the warehouses. On Saturday, they also involve themselves in the work of the Oratory, the meetings of the Employees' Group from the Formal Work Market and other activities.

155

Children take charge

In giving the more disruptive children more responsibility, the Ver-o-Pêso educators were rewarded by a new development that promised to increase the solidarity of the group. One lunch time, they announced that they had to go to talk to Graça about the erratic supplies of bus tokens. They would not be able to accompany the children to the restaurant. What was to be done about that?

"Put me in charge!" cried one periodic troublemaker. *"A good idea,"* they responded. *"But let's elect who will be in charge."* Two of the older children, including the one who proposed himself, and a younger child were duly elected.

The report-back from the cook - herself a former educator - about lunch was that all went well; if anything, more smoothly than usual. There was no throwing of food. All the children quietly washed and stacked their own plates. The following day the educator asked if they would like to continue to supervise lunch. They said they would and opted to elect supervisors from among themselves on a weekly basis. This was a new phase in the development of the cohesion of the group.

Work with children on the brink

The São Brás team of arts educators sets off in the late afternoon to meet street children. These children are generally from the least resourced and most damaged of families. They come to the streets through family catastrophe or a process of negligence and rejection - a progressive severing of bonds with the people closest to them, their schools (if they ever got to school), their community and ultimately the public at large.

On the streets they run greater risks of abuse and victimisation than working children. They are more vulnerable to manipulation by people in criminal activities, to the attentions of paedophiles and other damaged and damaging individuals and they are more exposed to violence and abuse from the police. Some people try taking them home as unpaid domestic workers. Sometimes well-intended but misguided people invite them home with the idea of rescuing them from street life. In most cases those who go find their way back to the street. A child from São Brás, taken home by a couple wanting to help him, seized upon their absence one day to invite all his street pals round for a party. They wrecked the house and then all returned to the streets. Many street children become involved in glue sniffing and other drugs and get drawn into prostitution and criminality.

People fear and, at worst, treat them as vermin. Apart from the more systematic killing of children by death squads in some cities, there have been cases of people pouring fuel over children sleeping in the street and setting fire to them. A boy the São Brás team works with was the victim of just such an attack and can no longer speak properly. The stand-off between society and its rejected children was starkly represented by a boy in his early teens. Shoeless, his clothes blackened with dirt and his hair matted, he backed along a Belém street away from a clutch of angry shopkeepers after some incident, real or imagined. Erect, light on his feet and expertly weighing in each hand a stone the size of a golf ball, he kept them at bay like a cornered animal until he reached a side street. He then bolted down it as fast as he could go.

For the child on the streets there are three types of people, says arts educator Carlos Roberto Ramos. *"Those who approach them to exploit them, those who intend them some violence, and those whom they can rob or exploit. We want them to recognise a fourth type - those who really want to help them and guarantee their rights."*

In the tradition of the Republic, the educators offer a respectful and affirming relationship and dialogue with them about their lives. But unravelling the social process of such extreme neglect takes time and determination. There are many impediments to be overcome in the expectations of both educators and children, as well as in the street environment in which the child continues to live. There are also simple financial constraints. Success is hard won. Few organisations and few individuals take the job on in a serious way.

When the São Brás educators began their work, some were frightened by the children's violence, but they came to realise that much of it was display. It was not just that bravado is part of the street child's survival kit. In moments of misgiving, such children may dump on the educator the emotional load they associate with people at whose hands they have suffered abuse - a policeman, their father or mother, a neighbour. The educators daily confront the violence inherent in the social system that tolerates the abandonment of a large segment of humanity.

157

"If you become a father figure and the real father beats them up, it can be very ambiguous," says arts educator Carlos Roberto Ramos. *"They challenge me, look me in the eyes and say, 'You! Beat me up! If you have the courage!' They test us to establish our limits, because their parents went from one extreme to another. They beat them up and threw them out of the home but they didn't explain to them why. We do explain ourselves. But this explaining can also be very tiresome to them, because they are used to receiving orders in a physical and violent way. Sometimes our words are like aggression because explanations are not part of their framework. They ask themselves - 'Why does this educator talk with me all the time instead of hitting me - even though I kick him and stamp on his feet?' When it is a teenager challenging an adult, the relationship is like a tug-o-war."*

"They can threaten one moment," confirms Ana Monica, another of the São Brás team. *"At another they want us to hug them, and cradle them in our laps and give them lots of affection."*

Newcomers to the work are commonly wrong-footed by the children, mistaking for instance a demand for respect for insolence. A good example is provided by Nara: *"If a child tells you, 'Fuck off!', it's because they feel you are interfering or threatening them in some way. The intention is not to offend you. It's a warning - 'Listen, you are not showing me enough respect'. Instead of taking offence you have to work at understanding how the child is seeing things."*

"Even when we have established a more trusting relationship they continue to test us," says educator Carlos Roberto Ramos. *"They may swing between aggression and seeking forgiveness. Some of us came to this work with ideas about building complete trust. We soon had to discard that. What we now look for is trust within a particular initiative or undertaking. Within that framework I try to demonstrate that I am there with them, but I have my rules and limitations which I want them to respect, as I respect theirs."*

Only by establishing an element of trust can the educators hope to get beyond the shield of compensatory thinking with which the children protect themselves from the full import of their circumstances.

Many street children insist that they *chose* to leave home, though choice is among the opportunities least available to them. They make much of the 'freedom' they enjoy on the streets. They refer to other street children as their family and some speak appreciatively of the city as a mansion with many rooms. In Belém, Ver-o-Pêso is their kitchen, where they get a variety of food undreamed of at home from people they call their clients - food discarded by restaurants, take-aways and stall holders, or food they steal. The city's squares are their rooms and bathrooms (some have ponds and drinking fountains) and they refer to São Brás, where they hang out, as the living room.

"Its great here," says one street child, who had come to Belém from cities in the south, adding like some touring gourmet: *"The food here is fantastic."* The home they left may be no more than a tiny wooden box at the end of an interminable, muddy, potholed track between other tinderbox houses, or a ramshackle structure clinging to a busy roadside or polluted river bank. But if every child condemned to live in such an environment abandoned their home or was abandoned, the pavements would be awash with children. The fact that they are not is in part a tribute to the enduring humanity of the millions of people made to live in poverty. Conversely, it also partly a tribute to the courage of some of the children who do leave home.

What makes children leave home is that their families' capacity to care for them and assure them of a future has been destroyed. A study of the families of street children noted a profound and disturbing sense of emptiness in some of their homes, and that, however horrendous the experiences of the children, they were generally more than matched by the experiences suffered by their parents, usually their mothers[8]. Where the home is abusive it is the more adventurous children who leave; the less so are more likely to submit to the abuse than risk the dangers of the streets.

"In a slum the children who come to streets are just another statistic," says arts educator Ana Monica. *"In the streets they are outstanding. They get plenty of attention, whether it be an act of aggression towards them or someone offering them food. They also get a sense of belonging. Most of them belong to a group or gang in which they have a strong sense of solidarity, friendships and companionship. Two very important things to them are glue and food. Friendship is more important because they will share the smallest portion of food."*

The friendship of the streets, however, is the camaraderie of outcasts who must also necessarily be predators. *"It is not the kind of solidarity we work for - that*

---

[8] *Identification of Characteristics of Family Dynamics of Street Children and Underemployed Families*, FLASCO/UNICEF,1991.

of people at peace with each other," adds Carlos Roberto Ramos. *"It will not lead them to demand better conditions. It doesn't imply respect for each other. Sharing food and glue at one moment is no guarantee they won't fight or take advantage of each other at the next. It is an exchange of favours - you must be on my side because I have been on yours at other times. If we assume, on coming into this work, that because they have allowed us to enter their world they will automatically offer us the kind of solidarity we value, or even do anything we ask - we are quickly confounded."*

The educators must contend with many environmental and circumstantial impediments to building relationships with street children. They are on the streets officially for only six hours a day, though they often work longer hours. For the rest of the time, the children are exposed to quite contrary influences.

Not least of the problems are charities and organisations with conflicting approaches and sometimes ulterior motives offering some kind of attendance to street children. They include born-again and other proselytising groups, some of which fill the children's heads with dreams of paradise in the after life but do little for them in this one. Others simply distribute various items - clothing or food. Some organisations seem to set out to create dependency, perhaps the better to acquit themselves with donors in terms of the numbers of children they attend to. Some are prepared to trick the children into doing what they want. One, for example, promised a boy he would get to play in his favourite football team if he went back to live at home. No doubt recorded among the organisation's success stories, the boy was back on the streets within days. These less demanding interventions can interfere with the efforts of the arts educators to provide the children with a sustained educational experience that will both give them insight into their circumstances and open up new choices for them.

The children's great mobility is also a problem. Individual children may vanish from the street for any number of reasons. They may also take off in groups. At the time of the research for this book many in the São Brás group had temporarily vanished from the terminal area. The educators had suspended activities to go to look for them. They were both concerned about them and questioning the value of their work with them. Despite the provisions of the Children's Act, there were still occasional roundups by the authorities. The children might also have moved to escape someone they feared. In the event, they had simply been attracted temporarily to some other part of they city. Whenever the educators know a child is in the hands of the police, they check that there are legal grounds and that proper procedures are followed. When a child is sick, they ensure he or she receives medical attention at hospitals or clinics that might otherwise turn the child away. If a child is beaten up, arrested or left unattended in an emergency, it is when the educators are not with them. The educators invariably try to follow up disappearances, but there is little they can do if a child takes off to another city.

The educators find imaginative ways to attract the children into group activities and engage their attention. One Christmas they proposed making a play about the birth of Jesus. *"Day after day the children came to discuss the story of the birth and play,"* says educator Dorotéia. *"Three kings had brought Jesus gifts. So we asked the children what gifts would they like to get? One would say a bowl of porridge, another a house to live in, and so on. So these were the gifts given in the play. We asked them, 'If Jesus was born today where would it be?' 'On the pavement!' one would say. 'Yes, in front of a hospital.' 'You mean Joseph would be told the hospital was full?' 'It would be closed by a strike.' So that is where their Jesus was born. And who should play Mary? It happens, they chose a gay adolescent. Then, on the day of the play, one of our three kings was arrested. The children immediately provided a stand in, so keen were they to see the product of their work. In another play, a dog was trying to catch a mouse and, when some disaster befell the dog, the mouse ended up helping him. As we make these plays up with the children, we discuss all the related ideas and feelings and relationships they deal with, as well as the things that happen in the course of making them,"* says Dorotéia. Simultaneously, the children experience a new creative, collaborative and loving relationship that encourages their continued involvement and starts to build their sense of self worth.

In other projects, the children have learned to walk on stilts, make masks, and perform folkloric dances and *capoeira*. All activities are held in the evenings in a square near the terminal. To have a discussion, the children and educators simply sit in a circle on the pavement under a streetlight, ignoring the odd inquisitive stare from a passer-by. At one such impromptu meeting the youngest child pulled a strip of cardboard alongside Patricia Cordeiro, the co-ordinator of the night team, and snuggled up beside her under a grubby cloth, his head in her lap. He was Marco, aged eight. His brother was 11-year-old Max, who had already been on the streets for four years. They were from the inland town of Castanhal. *"We left home because my father used to drink, come home and beat me up. I have brothers and sisters - they also beat me up,"* says Marco. Did he ever go home? *"I go to see my mother once in a while."* Many street children speak poignantly of the caring they once had or feel they should have had, usually from their mother. A number of those in the circle were sniffing glue from plastic juice bottles. Four of the group were girls, in their early teens. The eldest - a plump babyish 14-year-old - was heavily pregnant. The educators talked with her about where she would have the baby. They promised to help with baby clothes donated to the Campaign of Emmaus donations. Socorro, the social worker from the Republic had been alerted to her situation.

Cláudia, a newcomer to the terminal, joined the group for a while. Pretty, boyish, the 11-year-old had run away that same day from a state boarding school after jumping a wall. She had been sent to the school when foster parents, who had beaten her frequently, finally gave up on her. The school was a prison, she said. After escaping, she had hitched a ride to Belém on a truck. Though new to the city, she took nonsense from no one, seeing off older boys who molested her by slapping them sharply with a home-made car-tyre cosh she drew from her waistband.

At one point two powerfully built young men, end products of the street child's life, joined the group. *"These are our family,"* said the eldest, indicating the children. *"For us there is no other family. I spent my life on the street and now must take care of the young ones. Today many people are well off, but we who live on the streets survive every way we can, even by doing bad things."*

"My past it is very sad - so I won't tell you. Only God knows my past," said the other. *"Anyway I've been arrested many times and each time I came back to the street. Now I am big I want to go back to my home, but I like only my mother. My father is a corporal in the Military Police. Sometimes in the streets we get high on drugs and do crazy things - even kill people. But we are human beings and don't want to be treated as animals. I know we are wrong, but I still don't want to be treated like an animal. We do rob people - but why doesn't society help us? We have to do these things to eat."*

The two men began to dominate the conversation of the group. Such intrusions are hard to prevent when you work in public places. To shake them off, the educators moved away through the terminal area with the children, joined by others on the way. *"We know they trust us because they confide in us about things they would not otherwise - drugs, police violence, sexual diseases and so on,"* said Ana Monica. *"They have even shown us their most secret place."* 'The Hole' is a dark, malodorous, rubbish strewn lot behind a hoarding right on

162

one of the busiest pavements. Access gained via a loose flap in the hoarding enables a child to vanish from the pavement without trace. Children duck in there after thieving, or mugging someone, or snatching a bag. They also go there to have sex and to relieve themselves.

Progress made in the work with street children

After two years on the streets around the São Brás terminal, the arts educators have established themselves as reference points for street children in the area generally and begun to work more intensively with a group of 15 children. They see positive changes in the way children relate to them and each other. They are able to involve them in co-operative games and other activities.

They have also had some specific if modest successes. As in all the movement's work with children, the arts educators working with street children try to establish contact with their families, drawing where necessary on the professional support of the psychologist and social worker from the Republic. They work to improve understanding between family members and explore the possibilities for the children's return home. They put the families in touch with what few community resources are available and try to strengthen mutual support within families. All are uphill tasks given the families' and the Republic's very meagre resources. The fact is that many families of street children lack even the minimal requirements to reaccommodate them. Though there is no official foster placement service, the educators develop what limited fostering opportunities there are. Despite the difficulties, ten children have returned to their homes and one went on to the Republic's Formal Work Market, working for the federal bank.

To strengthen its work, the Republic had tried to collaborate with other organisations working with deprived families in Belém and maintained a good relationship with the Spiritism organisation, Lar De Maria.

"When we started this work," says José Raimundo, *"The Republic made an agreement with several organisations. They would work preventatively with families in the communities from which the children come. We would work here - where the streams of displaced children from the slums run into the city. There were never enough organisations but things have deteriorated and today we are even fewer."*

Reviewing the first phase in arts education

As the first phase of arts education was due for review, the educators working with both street and working children had no doubt that they were capable of making progress but were also keenly aware of the limitations of their achievements and of some shortcomings in their own training. They were questioning whether the Republic needed restructuring to work with street children.

Arts education had been successful in attracting street children and building a relationship with them but the children were now ready to move on. Built up over a quarter of a century in response to working children, the structure of the Republic did not appear to work so well for street children. How, for instance, could the child still living on the streets hope to enter the Republic's Formal Work Market?

"Is he going to work in the bank and then go back to the streets at night and sniff glue?" asked Dorotéia. *"We had one child who was very keen to move out of the streets. He wanted to do a course in the POA. So we fixed that up. He was very enthusiastic. But then at the end of his first week he was arrested. It was mistaken identity. He was released but was too ashamed to return to the POA."*

When the educators tried taking street children to the Republic to play football, they had run wild, thrown stones at other children and damaged and stolen various items. *"We even had our colleagues in the offices shouting at us, 'Hey, get your children out of here!' as if they did not know how to relate to these children. But these same people have been educators!"* complained Dorotéia.

Ideally, additional premises were needed in São Brás where an intermediate stage between the streets and the Republic might be developed. But, as in Vero-Pêso, there were no reasonably priced premises and, in the recessionary climate, the Republic was already in financial crisis. While the educators were racking their brains for a solution, the decision had been taken temporarily to bar the street children from the Republic.

"The limitations are beginning to appear as a result of our work. Perhaps it is time to stop everything again as we did in the '70s and dismantle this structure which was made for one type of work and which is now confronted with something new," said Dorotéia. Patricia, however felt there was still scope for

the educators to constitute a more effective bridge between the street and the Republic. Voluntary organisations, she argued, always worked within severe limitations and just had to find ways to overcome them. If the educators established clearer boundaries in their relationship with the children, it might improve the children's chances of regaining access to the Republic.

As so often happens in the Republic, the children were about to remind the educators that they were also active participants in the relationship between them.

The children take the initiative

Led by 11-year-old Max, some children arrived on their own initiative at the gates of the Republic. Dorotéia, Patricia and the other educators they knew were not there, so they asked instead to speak with Iolanda, whom they had not met but knew to be in the co-ordinating committee.

Max asked her to let the group in to play football.

Would they be demanding lunch, too? Iolanda wanted to know. Lunch was over for the day. Last time they came and were told there was no lunch, they made a big mess of the place.

The group had already had lunch, said Max. Anyone who demanded lunch or wanted to make a mess could be sent away.

But who would send them away?

The group itself.

Did everyone in the group agree?

Each one agreed.

Then they could all come in - just for 40 minutes for football and a shower before going.

They did just that.

This was a remarkable development in children who, outside their relationship with the educators, had mainly experienced rejection and who had also been barred by the Republic. Going back, on their own initiative, negotiating a contract and then sticking to it was something new and gave the educators new heart. *"The whole negotiation was*

165

conducted with great maturity, in a way that had never happened before," said Dorotéia. "They all came in. They decided who would be responsible for the ball. They took off their shirts to keep them clean. They played football. They showered and left."

"When we started this work, we were asking ourselves how to make contact and establish a relationship with these street children," said Patricia. "Now we are a reference for some of them and know some of their families. Perhaps now for the first time we are seeing the development of a grassroots nuclei of street children."

Her intuition proved right. In the following year, the group of street children began going to Republic regularly until they were taking part in more systematic workshops three times a week. With this development their reliance on glue sniffing decreased and their identity as a group grew stronger.

Nara and the girls groups

Meanwhile, the Republic was also facing a new dimension to Brazil's social crisis - the appearance of a growing number of girls on the streets. In a culture where the girl's place is still firmly in the home, girls pay more dearly than boys in going to the streets and their presence spoke of an increasing erosion of family resistance to poverty. Street and working girls come under great pressure to submit to prostitution and so risk losing any respect or self-respect they might have had. Boys who succumb to criminality do not suffer the same disgrace. There are outlaw folk heroes for them to identify with and they can regard themselves as fulfilling some essential requirements of manhood - daring, courage, adventurousness.

"Boys don't have to worry if they are beautiful or not. You can be both ugly and a good robber. What matters for them is their chutzpah," says Nara, who began working with girls in the Republic in 1994. "Competitiveness between girls is reinforced every day by men and boys in the streets who remark on which of them has the most beautiful breasts, or whether they have a beautiful arse or legs. So it is a preoccupation in their own relationships."

166

Because girls are competitors they do not benefit from the companionship boys find in street gangs. They tend to be more lonely and alienated. They fret over who is prettier and they exhibit much more unresolved jealousy than boys.

"If boys fall out and have a fight, the smaller one can say to himself, 'Well, I was beaten this time, but one day I'm going to eat that big guy up' - even if its only hurling a stone at him and running away. So it's over. When the issue is beauty, there is no way to pay back the girl who is prettier than you. So girls bear grudges. A girl is more likely to say she won't join a group unless another is taken out of it. We have to appeal to her to rethink, because the group is there for the other girl, too. When we go into the matter we find a history of fights and unresolved resentments between them.

"So the work is slower and very different from working with boys. There is a lot we need to understand much better in encouraging their participation and organisation," says Nara. In working through such issues with the girls, Nara identifies closely with them, having had to deal with similar problems herself.

Girls' groups began to develop only a few months before the research for this book was undertaken and was at a very early stage[9]. Two groups were being formed - one for under-twelves and the other for older girls. Each met at the Republic for four hours twice a week, in addition to joining the other mixed activities - such as lunch and recreation. Some were also in the Ver-o-Pêso group. A special large open-plan room was being prepared for them. Of 21 girls in the younger group, 15 were living on the streets and had no relationship with their families. The youngest was just nine years old.

As in all the work of the Republic, the aim was to awaken the girls to other social experiences and opportunities than those accessible to them. A major emphasis in the early phase was the building of their self-esteem through the relationship with the educators and each other, as well as the generally therapeutic environment of the Republic.

However pitiful their story, Nara treats street girls, not as pitiable, but as fellow human beings and as friends. *"They are very quick to figure you out if you fake friendship,"* she says. *"They have a word for it; they call you an 'artist'. It's fashionable and very easy to talk about street children; developing a*

---

[9]There are other organisations in Brazil which have done important pioneering work with girls. One of the first to do so was the Passage House in Recife.

relationship with them is quite another thing. Their extreme defensiveness makes it very difficult." Younger girls present special difficulties. Many of them are so distressed - and their heads so filled with the frenzy of the street - that they find it impossible to settle to an activity or a discussion for more than a few minutes.

Among the activities being explored by Nara and the girls was a dolls' workshop. Broken dolls of different types, collected by the Campaign of Emmaus, hung in varying states of repair in columns on the walls and there were bins of materials and spare parts. The girls and Nara sat together talking and repairing. The girls lavished great care on the work, possibly expressing the care they would like lavished on themselves, and they were proud of their workmanship. The atmosphere was relaxed, companionable, secure. At times the girls sat in a circle to discuss a particular issue - health, sexuality, relationships, their dreams, their families, street life, children's rights - based always on the girls' own experience. Periodically, a sale of repaired dolls was held, the money going to girls, making it easier for them to take the time out from earning a living.

Nara was also experimenting in trying to reunite girls with their families - particularly the younger ones. "*You can't give a child of 11 occupational training. So what is to be done with them between now and when they are old enough for us to do something with them, like admitting them to the POA of the Formal Work Market?*" she asked. "*This is the big problem we are trying to find answers to.*"

As with street boys, family reconciliation was generally hard won. Many of the girls were from homes where the father had died or abandoned the family. Typically, the mother was overburdened with responsibility, lonely and subject to extreme stress. She might well have a partner who resented the children. Lacking control over the crucial elements of her life, she might try to protect her children by being excessively punitive towards them. Nara negotiated an agreement between one mother and her 12-year-old daughter who had already left home and was becoming involved in prostitution. The girl agreed to return home if her mother stopped beating her. Within a week the agreement was in difficulties. "*She's not beating me with her fists but she beats me all the time with her words. I can't stand it,*" protested the girl. "*What do I do now?*" asked Nara in exasperation. "*Ask the mother to stop talking to her daughter? Impossible!*"

There were no suitable institutions to refer street girls to and most of the girls were unwilling to leave the streets. *"They say that despite the violence of the streets they will never starve there. They dream of living in a house but the concrete reality for them is the street."*

Three girls in the older group had proposed setting up house together. The Republic was considering that idea, which had been tried in other programmes for girls, such as the Passage house in Recife.

As with the Formal Work Market and the POA, a condition of the girls joining the groups was that they attend school. *"Most of them are now making an effort to attend school, though they don't all manage it every day. We keep telling them, 'If you don't go to school, you can't come here', but they know we are not going to throw them away,"* says Nara. *"If at 14 they have reached grade three, they will be able to go into the Formal Work Market. The idea of a real job, one that isn't humiliating, is a great incentive."*

The girls are also offered more structured education about health and sexuality, as well as play therapy and counselling. The older girls in particular are generally very keen to learn about health measures, their bodies, pregnancy and contraception.

Support for the street educator

Over the years, the work of the Movement of the Republic of Emmaus has attracted increasing support from professional people in Belém, especially from the university. The educators now go into the work better trained and with more knowledge than their predecessors. The lawyers, psychologists and social workers who reinforce them in their work have themselves to go through a learning process. In the Arts Education Project, for instance, social worker Socorro and psychologist Cláudia underwent the same training as the educators and so ascribe to the social and spiritual goals of the movement. They had to dismantle the professional/commercial orientation acquired in the course of their own education. Instead of being accumulators and traders of specialist knowledge, they learned to become sharers of their knowledge and collaborators in the effort to bring about a society that is respectful of human lives. They also now regard themselves as involved in a two-way educational process with the educators, one that echoes the exchange between educator and child.

Instead of regarding children on the streets as the problem products of problem parents - a view that often goes unchallenged in the US and UK - they ascribe their difficulties to the complex mesh of social relationships that conspire in denying human rights to the underclass. Rather than strive to integrate them into the 'excluding' society, they deploy their professional skills proactively to give them an experience which will lead them to challenge the process of exclusion.

"We are concerned with all the relationships - between the educator and child, educator and educator, child and child, and child and family," says Cláudia, who began working with the Republic as an extension student. She and Socorro divide their time between the teams, going with them to the streets, observing their work, participating in their evaluations, providing them with feedback, and accompanying them on home visits. They also provide counselling and therapeutic support to the educators, individually and as teams in handling the many stresses of the job - whether it be a particular incident, such as a violent encounter, or more general misgivings about the value of what they are doing.

"We believe it is the right of each child to be loved, respected and valued," says Cláudia. *"What removes these children so far from the rest of society is poverty. We are only a small group. Sometimes we feel we are too idealistic, but we also know that only by struggling with our politicians, with the government, and with society as a whole, have we any hope of changing this situation."*

The professionals constitute a third tier of people exposed to the transforming experience offered by the Movement of the Republic of Emmaus and, like the educators and the children, are likely to become agents of change in whatever avenues of life to which they proceed. Aware that they are helping relocate professional practice within a human rights framework, Cláudia and Socorro are keeping a systematic account of their own work and that of street educators.

Increasingly students are joining the Movement of the Republic of Emmaus on extension from the university to study the work of the educators, about which little written information is so far available. Lecturers from the university and popular university, UNIPOP, also give workshops to help the members of the movement think through the implications of their new relationship with government.

Medical back-up

Among the professional people who supported the work of the Movement of the Republic of Emmaus in recent times is Dr Conceição Costa, a paediatrician and university lecturer who first heard of the movement on joining the staff of the university in Belém. From a poor background herself, she undertook to establish a medical service for the movement, using prize money she gained in winning a major scholarship.

"If we don't do this kind of thing our society will disintegrate," she explains, reflecting a view held by other professionals in Brazil who choose to ally themselves to the struggle of the underclass. At first she came to the Republic once a week and was then asked by Padre Bruno to become an Affective Member of the movement.

She devotes four hours a day five days a week to the service which provides curative and preventive medical and mental care and produces research. She has established a small clinic at the Republic where she heads a young multi-disciplinary team including a psychologist, gynaecologist, paediatrician, pharmacist and a biochemist, nurses and assistant nurses, as well as a part-time dentist. The clinic dispenses among other drugs, low-cost herbal remedies grown by the Production Unit at the City of Emmaus. All involved have a strong sense of social commitment and accept low salaries. Running cost are low and the unit is small and simple.

"Our primary goal is to build the self esteem of the children and adolescents we see, through our respect for them as individuals," says Conceição. *"We work to improve their health and their attitudes to sexuality and to foster responsible sexual behaviour. We educate adolescents about contraception, both to reduce the incidence of pregnancy at an early age and to control sexually transmitted diseases. We also work on improving the general health and nutrition of children and adolescents and to improve the parenting skills of pregnant adolescents."*

The unit collaborates with the educators in the Republic and those at the school and Production Unit at City of Emmaus. It participates in formation classes of the Formal Work Market, the School and the POA, making inputs about health and sexuality but it also has its own educators who work one to one and with groups. Nara's girls' groups attend the health unit twice weekly for play therapy and education sessions with psychologist Ana Lúcia Cordeiro.

Employing group dynamics and imaginative games, she helps the children to explore ideas about relationships, hygiene, aspects of health and sexuality. *"These girls encounter a lot of violence. So before we work with the physical issues, we work to build their self-esteem helping them to respect and love themselves,"* she says. *"We want them to learn what it means to be loved and valued here and to love and respect each other - because that is the basis on which they can develop a critical awareness about their lives. We hope when they leave this place they will be multipliers of their experience here."*

The unit works both with children and their families, helping them recognise and overcome patterns of exploitation in their relationship. *"The parents beat the children and then, when the children start earning, the mother will stop working, expecting the child to take responsibility for her. We generally ask parents or people in the parental role to come here and work with us. We want to encourage a family relationship in which the burden of survival is shared and there is a mutual respect for rights and duties."* The unit also informs educators about issues related to health and sexuality - including attitudes to contraception and abortion.

Dr Conceição Costa involves a number of her medical students, as well as some dental students, in the work. The aim is similar to the involvement of law and social science students in the work of the CDM - to draw on their skills but also recruit them into the struggle for social change. The students are usually postgraduates and the numbers are kept small. The health unit also tries to encourage the development of similar services in other organisations such as clinics in poor districts, education centres, non-government organisations and government institutions.

Legal support

The movement's Children's Defence Centre (CDM) continues to give legal support to the work of the educators but also acts independently. Its multi-disciplinary team tackles cases of violence against children, and represents children accused of offences. It campaigns for the implementation of children's rights and raises public and media awareness of rights related issues. It advises on the setting up and development of the new Tutelary and Rights Councils.

Because of the overwhelming number of offences against children, the CDM gives priority to graver cases - murder, sexual abuse, rape and battering of children - and to those likely to have the greatest political impact.

For instance, it took up the case of a boy who was allegedly forced by a policeman to swallow live bullets. It pressed for investigations into the deaths from malnutrition-related ailments of eight young children in care and the castration and murders of seven young boys in Altamira. At the same time, it was probing separate cases in recent juvenile court records of six adolescents murdered while under police investigation. The only action that appeared to have been taken following their deaths was that the files were closed. The CDM wanted to reassure itself that there was no link between the killings that might indicate the operation of a death squad in Belém. In another initiative, the CDM was investigating the alleged traffic of children for prostitution in some of the state's mines. The situations it was unearthing were pitiful. In one inland town, batches of girls in their early teens were said to be assembled periodically in a square to be taken away by bus, ostensibly to work to help their families. In fact they were destined for brief lives as sex slaves in mineworkers' compounds.

The CDM works by publicly denouncing infringements of children's rights and pressuring the authorities to investigate alleged offences. It exposed alleged police malpractice in São Brás. Instead of following proper procedure, certain policemen were allegedly taking children they detained to a room in the terminal known as Heaven, where they beat or sexually abused them before releasing them without charge. The exposure led to a police inquiry which it was hoped would end the violence. In the Altamira case, the CDM was assisting the prosecution, acting on behalf of the parents of one of the victims. The CDM now operates its own research unit and documentation centre and is linked by computer to a national databank recording offences against children. It is also represented on the national Forum DCA, is affiliated to the National Human Rights Movement and a member of National Network of Defence Centres for Children and Adolescents. The growing involvement of Defence Centres, along with other players, in ensuring the implementation of the statute, enabled the National Movement of Street Boys and Girls to reduce its involvement in that direction and concentrate more thoroughly on the participation and organisation of children.

Recently the CDM enhanced its ability to promote children's rights and denounce infringements by setting up a news agency. Run by professional journalists, the agency feeds stories to the regular media and other activist organisations from a network of stringers it has set up throughout Amazonia. It is proving a vital force in throwing light on the circumstances of children in

173

a region colonised by multinationals and other business interests, and known for the brutality meted out with impunity to landless labourers and others.

What is in it for the educators?

Educators work hard for very little pay. There are never enough hours in the day to realise the full potential of the job. For the most conscientious contact time with the children is just the core activity. Apart from the additional voluntary activities they take on in the Movement of the Republic of Emmaus, some are involved in the setting up and operation of the new Rights and Tutelary Councils and in the National Movement of Street Boys and Girls. In the latter role they develop policy, campaigning and other actions and form grassroots nuclei of the National Movement with children from different assistance programmes. They conduct workshops for the children and help them stage local, municipal and state conferences at which they can elaborate themes for the two-yearly National Meeting of Street Children in Brasilia. Educators also try to explain to the public what they are doing, the problems faced by children and the kinds of social change needed to make a real difference. Among other initiatives, the educators held a seminar with the Belém City Police appealing for collaboration in improving the experience of children on the streets.

"Before the Children's Act, various branches of the state determined how children should be dealt with," explains José Raimundo. *"Now it is having to change and learn from others. Meanwhile, we have to contend with critics who allege that the law gives children rights but demands no responsibilities. So we make a big effort to explain what we do through the media and by giving talks."* Educators are often asked to give talks to secondary school children and take up other speaking, debating and media opportunities. The workload related to children makes it difficult for them and others in the Republic to involve themselves as fully as they might in the activities of other segments of the popular movement - neighbourhood associations, unions, organisations of landless people, black people, women and the sexual minorities - of whose struggle they feel they are part. Not all the educators even find time to participate in the National Movement of Street Boys and Girls.

The work is physically and mentally wearying but, because it is not a service but a relationship that they offer the children, it is the emotional wear and tear that many find most telling. Along with the gains they make, they also confront day in and day out the waste of young lives filled with promise. They work towards social change in the long term, emotionally strung out in the present across the shortfall between what they want for the children they get to know and care for and what is possible, given prevailing social attitudes and lack of democratic control over resources.

"An educator came here from São Paulo where there are death squads operating against children. He said that he worked with erosion. We often feel the same, particularly on the emotional side," says Dorotéia. *"If a child falls sick we get her treated at the hospital, then what? It's back to the terminal. I cannot solve the situation by taking her to my home. And there are many situations like this. We go home in tears. It fills us with anguish to think what happens to these children when we are not around. I ask myself what is the use of our raising the self-esteem of a child who will not be valued elsewhere."*

Joe McCarthy, an educator who specialised in working with more violent children in the city of Recife and Olinda in North-Eastern Brazil, also regarded himself as working with erosion. He personally knows more than 50 children in São Paulo and Reçife who have been murdered by death squads or others.

But why take up the challenge? Why do the educators not content themselves with escaping poverty? Why not, as most people do, drop a coin in the charity box and turn their backs on the acres of ramshackle shelters that ring the city, ignore the appeals of discarded children and withdraw from the dangerous downtown streets into the seductive cool of guarded, air-conditioned shopping malls and high-security homes? After all the poor have always been there. Why fight what you cannot change?

Educators are often asked such questions. Their answers are varied but they reflect the belief that in taking personal responsibility for the quality of life of the community, in resisting the culture of indifference and setting out to replace it with a culture of love and respect they embark upon a process of self-actualisation that in itself creates a new social possibility. Through their struggle for the citizenship of the socially discarded child, they simultaneously discover their own citizenship and with it the hope of a wider transformation.

Patricia Cordeiro describes the process very clearly. *"I applied for this work because I needed a job and thought I would like it,"* she says. *"But in this work you end up discovering your own self. At the beginning you are very unconscious. You need work and this seems interesting, but you don't have*

175

much idea what it is you are going to transform. Then you realise that the abandonment of the children takes place in the framework of the wider abandonment of many Brazilians. And you are from this layer too, though you did have some advantages and they enabled you to survive the hunger, which is not only for food, but also for compassion and justice. I had a very bad school. But I did have a school. I have a very poor family. But I do have a family. And this child on the street has lost, or risks losing, all the links that I by chance maintained. So today the idea that motivates us is of these children discovering themselves to be citizens and beginning to assert their right, and that of other dispossessed people, to a role in society.

"Their families cannot do that for them. Some are even more abandoned than they. So it has to come from a group like ours that commits itself to this process of transformation. Once we know this, we become very political and see that what we are doing is right. Then Patricia the educator is no longer somebody who just plays with the child on the street but someone who intervenes directly and politically when someone beats up this child, or when this child rips someone off. Why do I do it? Because if people like me, who have had the luck to survive poverty and the opportunity to experience the lives of these children, fail to intervene, then, I wonder, how will this society ever change?"

Such educators do not accept that things cannot be changed. *"I don't believe most people are indifferent about human suffering,"* says José Raimundo, who left a job in an accountant's office to become an educator. *"I think they are just absorbed in other things, or they believe that the problems are so great that whatever they might do would be insignificant."*

A rescuer of dolphins

People who became educators with the Republic have backgrounds of social concern and activism. At the age of eight, Nara, a staunch companion of the girls she works with, was one of a group of children who tried to stop the netting of dolphins. *"We would beg the fishermen not to kill them,"* says Nara. *"Then we heard that dolphins disliked garlic so we would smear that over the nets. We even tried reporting the killing of the dolphins to the police."* Rebellious against authoritarianism, her next strike was against the tradition of wearing white to a first communion. *"I had a pink dress I really loved. It wasn't a question of the colour. I loved the dress and wanted to put the two things that were very special for me together. So for me it was always important to be and to do what I really believed rather than what I was told."*

At 15 she became involved in political movements and later the trade union movements. She worked voluntarily with children as a member of the Minors' Pastorate in a poor district of Belém. Her own experience convinced her that if you can develop a clear view of your role in society in your youth you can transform the thrust of your life in a way that is much harder to accomplish later. Her motivation in working for the Republic is her identification with the children, the pleasure of working with them and the idea of trying to make her own experience available to them.

Education for citizenship

In 1994 in the school at the City of Emmaus a group of children aged 11-13, complained to their teacher about his failure to attend classes regularly. He had been recently appointed to the school by the Education Secretariat and understood little of its educational approach.

He brushed aside the children's complaint, so they approached the headmistress. She listened to them but took no effective action. They then took the matter to the Co-ordinating Council of the City of Emmuas and asked for a general staff meeting to discuss the deterioration in teaching practice, something inconceivable in a conventional school. They got their meeting. *"In a movement like ours,"* commented Graça, with a smile, *"sometimes the adults are ahead and sometimes it is the children."*

The meeting contributed to a general awareness in the school that it was adrift from its fundamental purpose. Various factors had contributed to the situation. Some of its most experienced teachers had left coincidentally within short space of each other and their replacements had not taken readily to the school's demanding methodology. The pay and morale of government teachers generally was low. Many were holding down two or three jobs to survive. They were not interested in extra duties required by the school. At the same time, faced with a growing demand for places from the Bengui community, and not wishing to exclude children, the school had admitted more than it could handle, giving preference as always to the most disadvantaged. A school designed for 500 children was now accommodating 1,400. Newcomers did not receive the same individual attention as their predecessors. The Montessori method was not properly maintained. The pedagogical links between the School and the Production Unit had broken down and the dialogue between the school and community of Bengui was eroded. *"We had slipped into mass-production education,"* said Padre Bruno.

Awareness of these problems led to the kind of radical action that saved the Republic's street work in the '70s. All involved stopped to consider what was happening in their school and decided to rededicate themselves to its pedagogical goals and review its practice. The teacher whom the children had complained of said the review process had made him more fully aware of the school's philosophy and he wanted the chance to help make it work. He kept his job. Teachers who were unable to make such a commitment had to go. Measures were taken to reintegrate the school into the life of the community and rehabilitate the Montessori methodology.

The incident illustrates how organisations attempting a development or socially transforming role can easily slip into an emergency assistance response to social crisis, ameliorating rather than challenging the status quo. Even where self and group evaluation is an integral part of their work, they can become the victims of erosion and lose their way. What has repeatedly saved the Movement of the Republic of Emmaus has been its readiness radically to review its situation.

In fact both the children's intervention and the school's response were also a clear illustration that even in a down phase the school continued to achieve some of its crucial purposes. Children who took part in the action spoke at the time with great affection for their school and revealed a strong commitment to the idea of a just and democratic society.

A liberating school

"The Bengui is not even accepted as a district - it is called a periphery area," said Elizangela (then 12). *"But in this school they make a big effort to give us everything they can. We hold an Olympic Games here. The teachers make sure we can all take part. Another good thing is the week of Children's Day in October. We have a different work schedule, with many activities to celebrate the day. We can really let our imaginations run free. Also boys and girls are treated in the same way*

in this school and have the same rights. Football is usually a man's game but here the girls play too. We are equal."

"There are very few boys in my class so most of our team are girls, but they complicate the game and so sometimes we win!" said Leônidas (aged 15).

"St John's Festival is also very good. We learn all about it and how to do many different types of dances," said Monica (aged 13). *"We have a lot of freedom. They have such a very nice way of doing things here. It stays with us. It becomes part of our character."*

"This is a school that liberates us - we don't wear uniform and the classrooms are light and airy," said Leônidas

"In other schools, children are not given so much attention, nor are they asked what they think of how the school is working," said Elizangela. *"Here we can talk to the teachers about anything - even very intimate subjects. They respect us very much. Many children would like to come here because there are only three schools for the whole district - an elementary school and two secondary schools. We sometimes have special sessions when we discuss the orientation of the school, what needs to be changed in Brazil and issues like children's rights."*

"Our school is very concerned about children's rights. I think all the children here think about changing the situation," affirmed Leônidas. *"The school campaigns for rights and the teachers give us lots of ideas so that we can take that campaign forward. They give us a lot of strength. Our school tries to help the poorest children. It is the children from the poorest families who get to work in the Production School and go on to the Formal Work Market of the Republic."*[10]

"We are interested in children's rights because here in the State of Pará they have not yet been achieved. There are many poor abandoned children who do not get their rights," said Elizangela. *"And it is not only here. Our teacher asked us to do homework about our world, so I read*

---

[10]This approving observation was the more remarkable because Leônidas had applied to go to the Formal Work Market but lost the opportunity to a child whose family was more disadvantaged than his own. It was assessed, on several counts, that he would be more likely to find other ways forward.

an article about Somalia. I was very moved by it. Our world has been divided into rich and poor and, although the rich don't want to admit it, they rely on poor people. But the poor are just like them - they are equals."

Asked what they would say to children who had no schooling or went to less illuminating schools than their own, Elizangela replied: *"If I was telling other children who live in poverty about this school, I would say they should keep their hopes up, because when we are finished here we are going to help them change this situation. Even if they can't study here, they can join us trying to change the life we live today."*

"I would say this school is very good. It explains things very well. When we leave we will try to do everything we can to change our country," said Monica. *said Monica.*

Chapter Thirteen

The Fourth National Meeting of Street Boys and Girls

The Fourth National Meeting of Street Boys and Girls, held in October 1995, marked the 10th year of the National Movement. In the two preceding years, there was a growing determination among progressive educators in the National Movement to reinstate the participation and organisation of children as a major priority.

This concern was reflected locally in the resolution of the 1994 General Assembly of the Movement of the Republic of Emmaus to place the participation and organisation of children centre stage. In particular, it was recognised that the organising aspects of work had been somewhat overlooked in the training of the first batch of arts educators. This would be remedied in the training of their successors.

Local movements and organisations in other parts of the country had already taken similar decisions, leading to an intensified investment in the development of grassroots nuclei. The National Movement also initiated a three-year programme attempting to organise street children who were not involved in any assistance organisation. In a number of centres there were experiments in establishing nuclei in poor community schools. At the time, there was growing interest within the National Movement of Street Boys and Girls in the idea of establishing grassroots nuclei in poor community schools, starting with schools favourably disposed to the idea. In Belém, the City of Emmaus School was a likely candidate. Pupils there were already strongly in favour of the idea. *"If they formed children's groups in the classroom, I would like to participate,"* said one. *"We already form our own groups to talk about different issues and deal with some of the problems we have. If they began to form grassroots nuclei here we would put all our efforts behind it. I would do my best to stimulate more groups,"* said Elizangela, *"I would get the materials together to send to other schools to form other groups. We would form many groups. Maybe we could improve this country if we do that. Maybe the youth together can really change it."*

As preparations got underway for the Fourth National Meeting of Street Boys and Girls, the strongest groupings of grassroots nuclei in the country were not in Belém, where the idea had been pioneered. They were in centres as far flung as Santarem, inland from Belém, Recife, in the north-east, and São Paulo to the south.

Pará State, of which Belém is the capital, was represented on the National Committee of adolescents responsible for planning and organising the Fourth National Meeting by a girl in the National Movement in Santarem, Clébia. The murder of her brother, however, threw her family into crisis and she did not get to the meeting itself.

Marcos, from Recife, also nearly did not make it to the Fourth National Meeting of Street Boys and Girls. His life had nearly ended earlier when he was barely into his teens. He lived in a very violent *favela* near Recife where there was a death squad operating. *"They murdered six of my cousins and several of my friends,"* he says. *"I was threatened several times on my own doorstep. Once, they pressed a gun muzzle to my head. It hurt a lot. I thought they were going to push it clean through my skull."*

He survived not only to participate in the Fourth National Meeting, but to do so as a member of the National Committee. Whereas only children from Belém attended the First National Meeting as elected representatives of grassroots nuclei, most of the members of the National Committee for the Fourth Meeting were both members of grassroots nuclei and the elected representatives of state-level committees.

Marcos opened the proceedings, sharing the platform with Minister of Sports, Edson Arantes do Nascimento, better known as Pelé, senators and congressmen and members of the movement, and he acted as a narrator in a production staged by the children at the National Theatre representing the first 10 years of the Movement.

"I got into some bad things in my teens. If it wasn't for the National Movement I would be on the streets, or dead," he said, before giving his opening address. *"Today I feel very strong. I am no longer scared. I have learned so much through the other children I have met. The educators, Joe McCarthy and Iran, were always calling to me and talking to me. They were there right with me in my darkest moments. They kept saying to me: 'You have to learn to walk straight - don't get killed like your fellows.'"*

182

In his speech, Pelé told the children: *"The most important aspect I see here is your will to change things."* To inspire them, however, he offered examples of 'self-made' men who had risen from poverty to great personal power and wealth - himself and two others. He had started out as a shoeshine boy. The others - both heads of TV networks (one profoundly mistrusted by the popular movement) - had started out respectively as an office cleaner and a street vendor.

In a brief ensuing speech, Padre Bruno quietly counterposed the social change envisaged by the National Movement. *"It is easy,"* he said. *"for some to be successful in life alone. To improve the lives of everyone is more difficult. But our commitment is not to leave others behind us but to enable everyone to succeed and grow together. Only then will we make life better and more dignified."*

More than 1,000 children, aged 7 to 17, and educators had bussed into the federal capital, banners streaming from windows, from 24 of Brazil's 27 states to attend the meeting. Many had travelled days and nights across the continent-size country.

They put up at an army barracks - in itself an extraordinary circumstance; children from the rejected classes hosted, in the act of asserting their claim to citizenship, by the very institution which for two decades had systematically sought to crush the exercise of citizenship in Brazil.

Over three days, they debated in circus tents in a city park and participated in a variety of imaginative educational workshops - dealing with health, sexuality, media, dance, mask-making and many others. The themes and events of the meeting had been defined by them with the help of the educators in a two-year preparatory process. With the government reviewing education policy, discussions in the grassroots nuclei and among representatives elected to state and national planning committees had focused on the access of all children to quality education. All aspects of education had been debated. Universal access demanded more than a radical reform of educational policy and provision, including proper salaries for teachers. It required alleviation of poverty and new employment policy, if many children were not to be penalised by having to work to support their families. Other prerequisites were adequate health and housing provision.

The purpose of education was also considered, producing a new cry - for, education for citizenship - paying tribute to the approach developed by the educators. Conference kits handed to each child on arrival bore the legend - *"I want to be educated as a citizen"*. On the second day, the delegates demonstrated outside the Ministry of Education, declaring before a line of grim-faced security men that they would make the education they dreamed of a reality.

From there, they streamed down the grassy slope to the National Congress in a celebratory procession, variously beating drums, bearing banners, on high stilts, one astride a unicycle. Some were dressed as clowns or wearing fantastical masks or carnival and cultural outfits they had made in pedagogical workshops. They funnelled into the basement between gleaming banks of cars and along a tunnel, their drum beats bouncing off the walls. As they emerged into the main building, they claimed the space with a victory shout.

In the assembly hall, the Vice-President of the National Council for Children's Rights (CONANDA) summoned the senior government and elected non-government councillors to meet them. He then welcomed the children in terms that recognised the heroism of their struggle. The Vice-President was a representative of civil society on the council and the encounter exemplified the new alliance made possible by the Children's Act between activists inside the decision making citadel directly supporting and supported by activists at the city walls claiming their right to enter. *"We are here to congratulate you for the 10 years of your movement,"* he said. *"Through it you can teach society many things it has lost and assist us to make public policies. We want this opportunity of not only listening and receiving you but also of joining with you in a proposal to modify Brazilian society. Inspired by your energy - this yearning of yours for transformation and willingness to fight for it - we are going to commit ourselves permanently to fight for a better society.*

"CONANDA thanks you for this opportunity. Bring us your proposals and we will surely be your voice in the congress. CONANDA is working to change public policies for a new future for the rights of children. It is not easy but we will achieve it with the support of organisations like yours." The children's elected spokespeople - a boy and a girl - then joined the councillors on the platform and took it in turns to announce the demands[1]. They criticised the

---

[1] In fact these demands had already been documented and presented to the government for consideration in its framing of new education and health policy due to be ratified in the week of the Fourth National Meeting.

slow progress in the implementation of Brazil's children's rights legislation. *"Our rights are not being respected. We are here to demand education for all,"* said the boy. *"We believe that with our participation in the councils things can improve,"* said the girl. Representatives of each of the five regional committees of the National Movement also spoke before contributions were invited from the floor. Each pronouncement was rewarded with rallying cheers and drum rolls.

The children said they wanted to be better informed about what CONANDA was doing for them. It should produce a newsletter in language children could understand and the government should allocate TV air-time for Children's Rights Councils throughout Brazil to report on what they were doing.

"We want to launch a national campaign to form Children's Rights Councils in the schools and community," said a boy. Councils had still not been established in some states; CONANDA should prod those states into action. The children also wanted to know how they might participate directly in the Councils for Children's Rights.

Several delegates spoke of violence against children, one from the north citing the case of the boys who were castrated and killed in Altamira. *"There is a cover-up,"* he charged. *"We are not able to find out who did it. We want the government to track down the culprits and arrest them. Children should go to school to study and not be violated."* He also referred to a household survey conducted by the National Movement in the north which revealed how young girls were taken into prostitution and exploited as labour. A boy from São Paulo condemned the killing of children. *"We don't know how many children are being killed. It happens too fast for us to keep track of it,"* he said. *"They leave children like dogs to die in the streets. If we were in school these things would not happen to us."*

The Movement believed it was wrong for children to be made to work instead of going to school. *"We are here to say children should not be in informal work. We should be in school preparing ourselves for a proper job,"* said one child. *"We don't want children to be working in the streets. They should be in school studying for a better future,"* said another.

A boy from the north spoke of the educational problems of poor community children. *"Children from eight to 10 years old have to work for up to 10 hours a day. Then they have to study at night. But the schools are often far away*

185

from where they live and work. It's very difficult for them to get to school."
Delegates wanted quality education based on an understanding of the problems
of poor community children and designed to integrate, not exclude them.

They also wanted the housing and health provisions necessary for children to
be able to pursue an education and rejected the idea of separate educational
provision for children who were educationally penalised because they were
poor.

"We are not marginals (criminals)," said one delegate, *"but we are being
marginalised."* The government's own statistics showed that educational
provision remained grossly inadequate. The children wanted schools in the
districts in which they lived and there was an appeal for teachers to be paid
realistic wages so that they were not forced to hold down two or three jobs.

The demands, which had been documented and already submitted to
government, were welcomed and referred formally to the appropriate ministries
represented on the council. A report of the National Movement recording
known cases of violence against children and demanding effective legal action
was handed to the representative of the Ministry of Justice. A CONANDA
spokesperson recalled the Second National Meeting in support of the Statute
for Children's Rights then going through Congress. He congratulated the
children on their action. *"I want to say, we are very proud of you and what you
have done,"* he said. While the law as it stood did not allow for children to
stand for election to Rights Councils they could make representations and urge
the election of representatives who reflected the voice of their Movement.

The children's ownership of the meeting

Through each of their National Meetings children discarded by mainstream
society have contributed to the advancement of children's rights in Brazil.
Their First Meeting in 1986 helped make children's rights a banner for the
nation's struggle for democracy. The Second in 1989 exposed the killing of
children and stimulated support for the Children's Act in the congress. The
Third contributed to pressure for the implementation of the Children's Act.
The Fourth - in the meeting with CONANDA - constituted the first step by
organised poor community children in presenting their experience and
demands to the new National, State and Municipal Rights Councils and
demanding more accountability of them. It was also the first strike in
establishing the Rights Councils as a new focus for children's organisation.

"We thought at one time that the work on the Children's Act detracted from our work with the children," said Mario Volpi, Co-ordinator of the National Movement at the time of the preparation for the Fourth National Meeting. *"But it is because educators spent so much time on it and on the setting up of the Councils that the children began to take an interest and regard them as important."*

Other key features of the Fourth National Meeting were the emergence of grass-roots nuclei as the basic unit of the organisation of children within the National Movement and the launching of the principle of education for citizenship. The children were clear that that is what they gained through the Movement. *"We don't only look to the school for education; we look to the Movement. It is very good,"* said one.

Asked what she would do if there was no grassroots nucleus in her district, an 11-year-old delegate said decisively: *"No nucleo de base? I would go straight out and start one."*

Young delegates, observers and educators who had attended a number of national meetings, felt that the children's ownership of the meetings had steadily progressed, as their own democratic structures had progressed. A boy said of the Fourth Meeting: *"It was the best to date. There was more participation and we were clearer about our goals."*

For many children the highlight was the encounter with CONANDA. *"We put a lot of pressure on the council. It was great,"* said one child. But would the government really listen to their demands? Although still exhilarated by their action, few expected instant results. *"We shall see,"* responded one 12-year-old girl. *"This is very new. But you can be sure of one thing; we will keep on coming".* *"New government policies on health and education are being approved by the congress today,"* said a youth in his late teens. *"We must study them and see how best to press for their implementation. Otherwise they will be nothing but paper."*

The children's ownership of the meeting was also evident in many small incidents. A foreign observer, among those who eschewed hotel comforts to join the children and educators in the military dormitories, was protectively adopted by a street child. The boy packed his belongings away under his own bunk for safekeeping, accompanied him to the showers and made sure he got on the right bus to the marquees in the park.

187

As the days of the meeting passed, the participants signed each other's T-shirts as a momento of the new fellowship they had found. *"I am never going to wash this shirt,"* said one on the final day. On leaving the barracks for the last time a group of children and educators from the state of Ceara spread out to form a large circle around the tough young army sergeant who had supervised their stay. They sang a song greeting him as a new friend. Then they collapsed their circle inwards to surround him closely. Where was he from? From the north-east. That was why he was such a nice chap. And handsome too! shouted some girls. What was his favourite football team? His answer was greeted with a shout of approval. Some jokes were exchanged and they thanked him for taking good care of them; they were not used to being protected by people in uniforms. They touched something in the soldier that brought him to the brink of tears. He in turn thanked them for being such good guests. They had cleaned the dormitories well after themselves. They had given back whatever they had stolen. In general they had been friendly and courteous. What they were doing was very interesting. He was very glad to have met them. He would think and speak differently of children who worked and lived on the streets from then on. Some minutes later, in a salutary reminder that life is not so easy, he came to the bus to announce that a soldier's camera had been stolen and appeal for its return. Sadly the camera was not found.

Among the last of the children to board the buses revving up for their homeward journeys was an eight-year-old girl, who had come with the group from Ceará. She huffed and puffed laboriously up the steep steps, imitating an old woman climbing the steps to her home. At the top she paused with a look of huge pleasure before a chorus of hands and voices welcomed her into the bus. She exemplified the right of all children to feel that they belong and the success of the movement in giving children that feeling.

Her bus gone, all that remained was a settling of dust, the circus tents like an abandoned nomad camp, a handful of volunteers cleaning up - befitting remnants of an event held by people investing not in physical structures but the development of the human spirit. What was of greatest value was winging its way back in the hearts and minds of the participants aboard the buses heading to poor communities and city centres around the country, where the children would report back to their groups, their schools and their families. Doubtless too, through extensive media coverage, the meeting has left some residue in the Brazilian collective consciousness and made some impact on the country's policy makers.

"Next year," said Marcos, before he left, *"I will be 18 and so I will have to leave the Movement. But I will come back as a volunteer, to pass on what I have gained to other children. The educators are not paid to do this work in the National Movement, you know. It is the most brilliant thing in Brazil."*

Many young people like him in the Movement, on the threshold of adulthood, express a determination to carry the fight for a better society forward. It is the hope of the educators that they will do so, collaborating with and inspiring others in the many grassroots organisations also struggling to develop the exercise of citizenship within Brazil's underclass and with it the challenge to the excluding society.

In this sense, the Movement is contributing to a process similar to that played by the Basic Christian Communities in the late sixties and seventies in preparing the generation of militant activists who weakened the resolve of the dictatorship. The children for social change will be pushing for a thoroughgoing participatory democracy against those who would curb and manipulate western style democracy in their own or their factional interest.

"We are not contributing today so that children can raise their heads when they become adults," says Padre Bruno. *"We are contributing so that they grow up with their heads erect. That is why this new way of educating children is the greatest investment that we can make in terms of social change and it is why I believe in my work. It will yield people who over generations will really struggle for their citizen's rights."*

Adriano, a well-known educator in Recife, said: *"People subjected to oppression are schooled in oppression. This is a great social danger. Poor people who rise to power can be every bit as bad as the rich. We see it happen all the time and point it out to the children. What is important about this educational experience (in the Movement) is that it seeks to break the cycle of violence. One working class journalist told me that, in his contact with unions and community organisations and associations, he kept meeting people who had been in the children's movement. I believe that in future years many people who were on the streets as children will be actively and militantly engaged in the social process. They will have a very fine intuition for life, for what really matters to people and how to organise for a better society. I am sure of that. We will also see many people who have worked in the children's movement coming up through the system to stand for election as mayors and councillors. If that happens then I will die happily."*

At the time of writing there are 4000-5000 assistance programmes for children operating in Brazil. *"A third or so of these programmes has some concept of the participation and organisation of children,"* says Benedito dos Santos. *"If we talk about children from assistance programmes who also participate in an independent organisation like the National Movement this one third reduces to 100 programmes. This is the number which have become Associate Members of the movement since 1990[2]. In addition there are another 100 which have pedagogical and methodological affinity with the movement and the idea of children's participation and organisation is growing. Nowadays you cannot talk about acting on the behalf of children without listening to what they have to say. We are at a stage where we are seeing a rough draft of the child as citizen beginning to emerge in people's minds. I would say the greatest achievement of the National Movement in its first ten years wasn't the Children's Act; it was creating the historical possibility of children being politically active as a mobilised and mobilising force in society - creating it not just as an idea but in practice. This is a great contribution. Even though in terms of the number of poor community children in Brazil few are participating in this process so far, the historical possibility has been established."*

In Dos Santos's view, the children's meeting with CONANDA reflected the renewed emphasis in the National Movement on the participation and organisation of children. It represented the continuation of the strategy developed through the Movement's involvement in the mobilisation for the Children's Act and also indicated a new departure for people on the political left. The adults who had come into the National Movement from the left had abandoned the paradigm of attempting to seize power as the way to bring about social change. *"Now we see another way forward. We are living a process which we call negotiating democracy. We are playing the elite at their own game. So we continue to fight at the institutional level but we draw our power to negotiate at that level from the mobilisation of the people, including the children. That is what made the impeachment of President Collor possible - an alliance of people with power inside institutions who fight for social justice conjoined to the fight of those who are on the streets."*

---

[2] Having set out as a movement of individuals rather than organisations, the Movement in 1990 established an associate membership to organisations that employed the same methodology. They are active collaborators with the movement.

Chapter Fourteen

The Movement of the Republic of Emmaus turns 25

The Fourth National Meeting was the production of many people from many parts of Brazil. It was also a consummate expression of the fundamental conviction of the first youth group in going to work with children in the streets of Belém 25 years before - the conviction that there were shining qualities in such children which, demonstrated to the children themselves and to the public, would make it less easy for society to consign them to the scrap heap. In the month in which the National Movement celebrated its 10th birthday with the Fourth National Meeting, the Movement of the Republic of Emmaus, launched celebrations of its 25th birthday.

It did so by holding a birthday party in Republic Square in Belém for everyone who had been involved in it over the years whom it was able to notify. There was a large turnout. It also chose the moment to launch a new initiative that would ease its cash crisis and simultaneously strengthen its public education role. Instead of turning primarily to international funding agencies it offered people in Belém a more systematic investment in its work, creating a membership scheme by which they could make regular monthly donations.

A challenge for a movement like Emmaus, subject to the double flux of a changing membership having to adapt to an ever-changing reality, is that of keeping a true course. It is ever having to transform itself and has shown itself able to do that. *"There is nothing in the movement that is regarded as finished, nailed down, untouchable,"* says Padre Bruno. *"Everything can be questioned, everything changed. People are not always very ready to dismantle what they make. The trick is to work with something that deserves to be continually recreated. It's not only the movement that we regard as unfinished - it's also everyone of us who are in it. It is these features of the movement that are difficult to translate to an institutional, and particularly a governmental setting."*

What is continually recreated in the movement is the locating and rescuing of the essential humanity of the children, the educators and through them of the wider community of Belém. And to do this not by instruction but by a deliberate setting out to create affirming and loving human relationships, a sharing of dreams, within a socio-economic context that systematically dehumanises.

The context has changed dramatically - from the state and multinational capitalism under dictatorship to the neo-liberalism and national capitalism of the 'free' market era. The latter, with its promotion of individual opportunism over community interest, and its deification of competition as opposed to solidarity, has only reformulated the excluding society in a more chronic form.

Amid the diversion, glamour, false promises and seduction of the market, it is less easy for the young educator to discern what in the environment, and in their own make-up, works for or against their main purpose.

Members of the Movement of the Republic of Emmaus today are subject to many more conflicting appeals as to how to spend their time, what to value and what to do with their lives than they were when the choice lay simply between the oppression of dictatorship and the struggle for liberation. There is a wider diversity of experience and personal expectation among them. The intensified struggle to survive mitigates against voluntary action. The widening gulf between those who are plentifully and adequately supplied and the desperation of people in poverty, makes voluntary commitment to the latter an act of greater personal consequence for anyone who might otherwise escape poverty. The guiding truths, too, have become less accessible, with liberation theology besieged within the church, an erosion of faith in the church itself among the young, competition from reactionary evangelical churches and socialism still winged by the failed forms of Eastern Europe. Finally, the Movement's own inspirational leader, though still around, has stood aside. Some of its pioneers regret what they experienced as a diminishing of its spiritual core.

Bido Francisco, the current General Co-ordinator, does not recognise any such loss. *"The Movement was born as a church Movement,"* he says. *"It is no longer the case, as it was even 10 years ago, that most of the youth come to us through the church. When I was a boy, you would ask people, 'Do you want to become a priest or nun?' Many people wanted to. Today, nobody wants to be a priest or a nun. Georgina was my catechism teacher. She prepared me for my first communion. She is a militant of the faith. Today you don't have these kinds of people around. But I would not say that the Movement lacks spirituality. It just wears different clothes.*

"We are in a time where our dream is becoming more compromised because of the extreme need people are experiencing. I never tell visitors that everything in the Movement is wonderful. We know that the dynamic nature of our work means that we do not always make the best choice. Our Movement also contains deep contradictions, people for instance with very different orientations; professional people who may feel they can't go on a home visit without a car; educators who live the same reality of the children. Only yesterday a graffiti gang invaded the home of one of the educators, Ana Monica. Her brother is in an opposing gang and has now been arrested. It is a time of high unemployment, hunger and great violence and all of the social movements are more fragmented and weakened at the moment. We are part of this society and absorb its contradictions. What we have to do is to find better ways to manage the contradictions between what we aspire to and what we can hope to achieve at any given time."

Under its lay co-leadership, the Movement had been stepping up the training of its affective members and drawing on the support it built up over the years from within the university to increase its powers of analysis and deepen its knowledge of its historical role. It is considering appointing a council of external advisers, people close to the popular struggle with varied skills - including perhaps a political scientist, a lawyer, a priest, a social worker, a psychologist, a pedagogist. It is also considering moving the CDM back to its original accommodation, freeing the house at the Republic for the revival of community experiences. Padre Bruno has stood down as a member of the Municipal Rights Council and plans to leave the CDM to devote himself to the training and development of educators.

In another move to strengthen popular demand for children's rights, the Movement, working through the CDM, had made a start on encouraging adults in poor communities to form Children's Right Defence Committees, the first being established in the Bengui with four others in the planning stages. Its hope is to locate such committees in schools, with the aim of encouraging schools to become community resources and centres of community action, in the way in which the School at the City of Emmaus is conceived. It is organising community workshops to mobilise support for the establishment of the committees. Meanwhile various grassroots nuclei of children have been forming within the Republic, including two groups from among the street girls Nara worked with. They have taken to naming their groups in imaginative ways. The older girls, some of whom were already mothers, formed a group which called itself 'The Art of Living', while the younger girls named their nucleus. 'The New Song'.

One of the most welcome developments both in the State of Pará and nationally has been a clearer awakening of interest in the children's struggle by other branches of the popular movement which until a few years ago did not recognise its significance. The Trades Union Congress (CUT), the Landless Rural Worker's Movement (MST), residents' associations and others are beginning to engage in the Children's Rights forums and Councils.

The triumph of the mid '90s of the Movement of the Republic of Emmaus has been its emergence as one of lay people, overwhelmingly from the poor peripheral areas of the city, still able to attract young people, inspire in some a long-term commitment and in others an enduring concern for discarded humanity, mobilise public collaboration, welcome constructive criticism and look critically at its own work, engender new ideas, keep alive its dreams, carry the fight forward.

Physically, the Republic is a flat patch of swampy land, offering a scattering of simple buildings, two warehouses and a watery football pitch and divided by a polluted, malodorous stream. But the energy that emanates from it still reaches into the hearts of many people in the city and, through various networks, links up with activists against oppression in many other cities and many other countries. Just to step into the company of those who bear the Republic in their hearts and minds is to find yourself in a spirited world where you know you will be valued for what is best in you, in which your best self will flourish. Members of the Movement speak often of their dreams and preface their most ambitious ideas by expressing a doubt that perhaps they dream too far.

Are they hopelessly utopian? The answer must be 'no' - because they are also tireless workers for a reality many of us dream of; against all odds, they recreate it daily, not as an ideal, but as lived experience, proving that it does not take saints to do so. 'No' also, because between the world they strive for, and the nightmare they strive against, there is no choosing.